Jesus and the Family

Jesus and the FAMILY

Crisis and Conversion
in the American Household

FRANK G. HONEYCUTT

CASCADE *Books* • Eugene, Oregon

JESUS AND THE FAMILY
Crisis and Conversion in the American Household

Cascade Books
An Imprint of Wipf and Stock Publishers
199 W. 8th Ave., Suite 3
Eugene, OR 97401

www.wipfandstock.com

ISBN 13: 978-1-61097-907-8

Cataloging-in-Publication data:

Honeycutt, Frank G.

Jesus and the family : crisis and conversion in the American household / Frank G. Honeycutt.

x + 92 p.; 23 cm—Includes bibliographical references.

ISBN 13: 978-1-61097-907-8

1. Jesus Christ—Family. 2. Jesus Christ—Views on the family. 3. Families—Biblical teaching. 4. Families—Religious aspects—Christianity. I. Title.

BV4526.2 .H645 2013

Manufactured in the USA.

For my children

. . . in remembrance of their baptism days:

Hannah (10/20/85)

Marta (1/29/89)

Lukas (8/25/91)

. . . when you were buried with him in baptism, you were also raised with him through faith in the power of God, who raised him from the dead.

—*Colossians 2:12*

Acknowledgments

Many thanks to:

The Lutheran congregations I've served—St. Paul's, Trinity, St. John, Ebenezer, and St. John's—in various Virginia and South Carolina locales. These five congregations have shaped my understanding of the family of God in countless ways.

Dot Jackson, friend and fiction writer, who carefully read early stages of the manuscript.

Michael Kohn, who regularly helps separate the wheat from the chaff in my writing.

The Pannier People—Larry, Ed, John G., Barry, John H., Kent, Charlie, Dennis, J. J., David and Dale—whose annual week-long bicycle forays on the Blue Ridge Parkway have primed the writing pump in untold ways.

Cindy, who still puts up with me after thirty-two years. All I write and hope for is inspired by you.

Contents

1

Lost in the Woods

I LOST A CHILD in the woods a couple summers ago; came very close to appearing on the evening news. No kidding.

For close to twenty summers, I've taken youth backpacking for three-day trips in the Virginia and Carolina mountains. The most serious incident in past years was blisters. Well, I did misplace two young girls once for about ten minutes. They talked themselves right past our campsite. But this was different.

Boyce was in the middle group at the end of a long and hot day. Two miles from camp we took a break. I described the trail ahead to our leaders and led the way. An hour later we all piled into camp; no Boyce. Somehow he'd been allowed to go ahead of his group. I knew exactly where Boyce had missed a turn in the clearly-marked trail, but with afternoon turning to evening, it didn't matter.

I grabbed my cell phone (which of course did not work in the gorge where we planned to camp) and started running back toward the last road crossing. Unbidden, lawsuits and even memorial services danced in my head. Someone called search and rescue. We flagged down a car and a young woman took me back to another road crossing further north. With lengthening shadows, still no Boyce. I was very close to pastoral panic mode. Hours had passed since anyone last saw him. Evening was turning towards darkness. I'd read about how these things sometimes end.

The voice mail on my cell phone as we emerged from the low point on the forest service road was that of an incredibly calm mother who said, "Pastor Frank, they have Boyce at the entrance to the state park." I almost started crying. When we caught up with Boyce he was surrounded by state police, park personnel, and several serious search and rescue professionals. I'm still a bit surprised they were willing to relinquish the lad to his embarrassed and incompetent pastor.

Boyce and I got back to camp with zero light left in the day. The woods were absolutely black. We had a hard time making out the relieved faces of our church youth group in the dark. Boyce began to explain excitedly the events of his day to a mesmerized audience. I collapsed in a heap of exhaustion, finally remembering that we should give God thanks for all the remarkable events that led to one of our members getting found. Wandering over to the group in the dark, I interrupted Boyce's animated regaling and suggested we pray together. "Gosh, Pastor Frank," said the once-lost boy, now a bit irked. "*Can't you see I'm tryin' to tell my story here?*"

~

I've laughed and thought a lot about that irritated question since that crazy afternoon and evening. Even though it was offered by a sixth-grader, the question sums up a lot of postmodern impatience with the Bible and church tradition. Almost desperate to make sense of and share *ad nausea* the Facebook and Twitter details of our lives through cyberspace, there is also regular resistance, even among church people, to filtering our stories creatively through the older and wider canvas of scripture. The Bible, for many, cannot hold a candle to authentic personal experience. *Can't you see I'm tryin' to tell my story here?* We are finding, through agonizing trial and error, that our personal stories cannot alone withstand the weight of the forces of sin and darkness that seek to separate and break us apart.

Families in the United States today—fraught with divorce, teen depression, and a desperate search for meaning—are thirsty, whether they know it or not, for a story wider than their limited genealogy that makes sense and brings unity. Families need and want a way out of the woods when they become lost. Very often the desire to "tell my own story" (however compelling and interesting) fails to forge a trustworthy path leading to freedom and new life. We need an older guide. We need Jesus.

The challenge for pastors and biblically astute congregations is that Jesus says some downright strange and even off-putting things about the family, foreshadowed by how he seems to treat his own kin.

The chapters to come will treat these rather alien texts head-on. For many years I ignored these passages as preaching possibilities when they rolled around in the lectionary cycle—too strange and isolating, especially for families that seemed on the verge of breaking up. I've since concluded that Jesus's words on the family are key to understanding what he meant by the kingdom of God. If we listen closely, his "offensive" words about home life are the very ideas and teachings that can bring health to spouses and children who desperately search for a way out of the woods.

2

Jesus and His Own Family

Yes, I see them there. Two cousins sipping tea in the hill country (Luke 1:39–56), comparing notes about unusual pregnancies, water retention, hopes for their children, and promises from God. Two prospective moms. A mute old priest slinks around in the shadows: old Zechariah, struck dumb by an angel for innocently wondering how in the world an octogenarian couple could possibly get pregnant together. I imagine him in slippers, serving the women silently. It's just as well for Zechariah, for any man during a pregnancy, don't you think? Just listen, zip it, and get out of the way.

Maybe Elizabeth was old enough that she never lived to hear about her famous son, John the Baptist, call a whole assembly of religious elite a "brood of vipers," a pack of snakes. Perhaps Elizabeth was spared that little report from the river. I hope so. Moms want their kids to do well, but not to wind up in jail, as John did, even for the right reasons—headless, come to think of it, when he told the truth one too many times. Too much for any mom, I suspect. I hope for her sake that Elizabeth was resting with the saints by the time her baby boy went a little wild for God.

But how about the other mother? I love her mettle as the story opens. "She set out and went with haste to the hill country." Mary is excited. Let's say she pulls on her hiking shoes. She gains elevation. She's moving along at a pretty decent speed, sometimes gleefully jumping from rock to rock; maybe moving across a mountain meadow like Julie Andrews, arms open wide in rapture. Jesus is still a zygote inside of her, early in the first trimester, but she has to tell somebody.

With nobody around, maybe she rehearses her famous song that she will soon belt out in Elizabeth's kitchen: *My soul magnifies the Lord.* The Magnificat. A song so radical, so full of reversals and change, rich and poor trading places, that parts of the world (notably Brazil) have banned the song for the political unrest it's caused among the people. This song is so sure of what God is going to do in Jesus that Mary uses verbs that suggest it's already been done. Most of the verbs in the Magnificat are in the past tense. Mary senses the whole world changing inside of her. She cannot keep quiet. She cannot keep still. She pulls on her boots and hikes with haste into the hill country. I've always loved that about her.

Magnificat. Magnify. Magnification. Think of the magnifying glass you used to carry in a pocket to burn up a dry leaf or paper with the sun's rays. I used to try and lure my little brother into mayhem with my magnifying glass but he never fell for it. But a magnifying glass was principally used to make things larger. Mary's soul *magnified* the Lord; made God larger. Her own maternal soul did that.

The soul can be a dark place. My own soul, I'll be the first to confess, darker than most, often *minimizes* the Lord. On my worst days, I could sing the Minificat rather than the Magnificat. I'm wondering if this was also true of Mary at times.

Part of the truth of the Christian life is that baptism creates a whole new family—a family that magnifies the Lord and embraces this upside-down vision of the world of which Mary sings. John the Baptist, Jesus's little womb buddy back in Elizabeth's kitchen, would grow up and get it just right: "He must increase, but I must decrease" (John 3:30).

And Mary also had it right. "My soul magnifies the Lord." Her soul made God larger. But part of what I love about this woman is that she undoubtedly must have had days when she was not so sure about that; surely had questions about the song she rapturously sang in her cousin's kitchen. Even Mary. I like that about her. Because oddly, it gives my own fickle soul—forgiven through the cross, washed in baptism, fed in communion—the gumption and courage to take the next step. The next step in my own family's halting attempts to magnify the man. The next step as a husband, a dad, a disciple. The next step as one household of God living at a specific address.

≈

In Luke's Christmas story, most of the light (before and after the sacred birth) shines on Mary even more than Jesus. After the angels appear and frighten the shepherds; after they collect their wits, locate the stable, and share their news with the weary parents, Mary has a quiet moment in the margins of the story that's easy to miss, but may serve as an early key to understanding Jesus's theological take on the human family. Look closely. What is Mary doing?

"Mary treasured all these words and pondered them in her heart" (Luke 2:19). Mary "pondered" these words from the excited shepherds—which is sort of odd, if you think about it. An angel has already popped in on Mary prior to her happy dash to Elizabeth's kitchen and so she surely expected the rather paranormal nature of the birth out there somewhere on the horizon. But she seems rather surprised and taken aback by the shepherds' midnight tale. She treasures their words. She "ponders" them.

The Greek word here is *symballo*. It's where we get our English word "symbol." The stems in this word, broken apart, are *sym* ("together") and *ballo* ("to throw"). When Mary "ponders" here at the manger, she is literally throwing ideas together; ideas that had not been together in her thinking heretofore. Mary ponders. A related word is "parable," even though it's spelled a little differently than "symbol" there at the end of the word. A "parable," literally, is one idea "thrown alongside" another idea or image. Jesus, upon growing up, told these a lot in his ministry with marvelous theological friction and sparks occurring as a result of the encounter, the narrative toss.

Mary ponders. She "*symballo*-s" the words that she hears. She throws them together into her heart and they rattle around there, percolating with promise amidst the clattering of cows and sheep herders. The story does not say she "believed." Nor does it say she ran out into the Bethlehem night shouting, "Hey everybody! Look at me! I'm the lucky one! I'm the lucky girl!" No, Mary "ponders." For me it's a new place from which to consider Christmas.

Several years ago I ran across an interesting sociological study that I first heard from evangelist Tony Campolo. One hundred ninety-five year olds were asked a single question: If you could live your life over again, what would you do differently? One hundred older people at the end of their lives—what would you change?

As you might imagine, there were lots of answers to that question. But the answers were also amazingly similar, grouped into three consistent thoughts. These older people basically said three things: 1) They would *take more risks* and not live this life in such a safe way; 2) They would engage in work that would *outlive their time on this earth*, work that would continue to make a difference long after they were gone. But then they said a third thing. These 100 ninety-five year olds said that if they had another life to live they would all *reflect more*. They would slow down and think about this amazing world, the intricacies of breath and love and food and rivers; just being alive. They would all spend a lot more time in reflection—deep appreciation and wonder.

I once saw a wonderful photo in the museum of a Columbia, South Carolina, hospital, only a couple blocks from the church building where I served. I was visiting one of our members and took a little detour into the museum. There was an old picture (1926) behind the glass—a long line of nurses looking out at the camera on graduation day; fifty-nine young nurses in a long row (I counted them) in their starched uniforms and caps; all expectant and hopeful as they went out to serve their patients over eighty-five years ago, their lives completely ahead of them. Something new was beginning for these young women, the passage of time now a certain history for them, as time makes its slow march forward for us all.

Mary "pondered" all the words of the shepherds. She "threw them together" into her heart. The story reports that the very first moments of her life as a mom began by thinking, reflecting, wondering.

I find it instructive that Mary did not pick up her cell phone, so to speak, and contact mom and dad instantly with the good news. "He's here, mom! Eight pounds, seven ounces; brown hair, ten toes with an excellent Apgar score." No, Mary (certainly after some rest following labor and delivery) pondered the words of those who arrived breathless at the manger. She let it all slowly sink in. It matters a great deal what we choose to "throw together" into our hearts; what we ponder in the silence. The stories we tell—the stories that shape our imaginations—matter mightily in our rescue; the narrative from which we make decisions and plan our days; the images and bits of bread that lead us safely out of the woods.

The story that's really in our hearts, knocking around in there, will shape our days and ultimately define who we really are more than most anything else. When this baby Jesus grows up, he will utter one of the most devastatingly honest things anyone could possibly hear: "It is from *within*," he says in Mark's gospel, "from the human heart, that evil intentions come" (Mark 7:21). And, I daresay, all good intentions. Pondering is powerful stuff.

Kathleen Hirsch tells an Advent story[1] about her young son.

> I heard rummaging in the living room, then the metallic tinkling of ornaments on the lower boughs. Minutes later he was standing beside me, a solemn three-year old holding a stuffed red heart that he'd taken from the tree.
>
> "Mommy," he announced. "Pretend that I am Gabriel."
>
> I looked at the chocolate around his lips, the sleeves of his Henley rolled up for wings, and his utterly sincere and serious eyes.
>
> "Kneel down, Mommy," he instructed me.
>
> I obliged. Gabriel and I were face-to-face, inches apart, in front of the stove.

1. Hirsch, "Glimpse of the Holy," 10.

> "Mary," he addressed me. "You shall have a son. And this," he extended the plush red heart toward my face. "This is your holy."
>
> Here, he paused for emphasis. "You must carry your holy with you always, Mommy—even around your neck—so that Jesus will know that he is holy too."
>
> I looked at the heart offering, velvet and gold, resting in my hand. What to do with the hot coals of a prophet?
>
> Then, perhaps overcome by the force of his own inspiration, my Gabriel turned and fled back to the crèche to distribute more of the "holy" to the creatures assembled there.

Mary "pondered" all these things in her heart. She threw together the new announcement (and challenges) she was hearing from the shepherds with the promises she already knew in her heart—the old stories she'd heard since childhood. This was her "holy" (Isa 6:3), her calling; the song of the angels echoing down through the centuries from temple to starry field to manger, filling the whole earth with praise. Such pondering is indeed powerful stuff and can help us through the darkest woods.

~

We don't know a lot about the actual family life of Jesus. But children grow up quickly. In 1928, German artist Max Ernst painted "The Blessed Virgin Chastising the Infant Jesus before Three Witnesses." Jesus appears to be an older boy in the painting rather than an infant. Shockingly, Mary is spanking her son's bare and reddened bottom. She is maternally under control, wearing a form-fitting red dress, halo intact, as if about to depart on a date with Joseph. Jesus's halo is visible on the ground alongside his mom's bare feet, suggesting she's been interrupted in the getting-ready-to-go-out process. Jesus, naked and face down, squirms uncomfortably on her lap. It's not clear what her son has been doing, but Mary is decidedly unhappy with her little boy. The scene provides a lot to think about and take in. One of the three witnesses in the nearby window is Ernst himself.

I mention this painting because I like to think that even though Mary once pondered sweetly and privately about her soon-to-be famous son, she also lost it at times in family life as most moms are wont to do. Why wouldn't we think that Jesus tested the limits of parental patience as a young boy as he must have done later in life?

They were at this wedding once, remember? No wine. Tradition has it that Mary was in charge of refreshments that day (John 2:1–11). She leans over to her son; she's seen what he's capable of. Why not pull a few strings if she has them to pull? So Mom says, hopefully, "You know, they have no wine (wink-wink)." No need to call the caterer, right? Do you remember what Jesus says here? He makes it right in the end, but do you recall what he says that day to his own mother? "Woman, what does that have to do with you and me?" I would never have gotten away with calling Ruth Honeycutt "woman" at 6939 Hickory View Lane in Chattanooga.

Then there's the incident of that little vacation trip to Jerusalem (Luke 2:41–51). Jesus is twelve; precocious and wise beyond his years. But he gets lost. Or so everybody thinks. At age four, in 1961, I got lost at the beach for a couple hours (reminiscent of our friend Boyce) and I'm told my mother ran straight into the ocean; she was in such a state. Jesus was missing for three days. *Three days*. Some may see symbolic foreshadowing here. Mary and Joseph felt only panic. When his parents find him, do you recall what he says to mom and dad? "Why were you searching for me? Did you not know that I must be in my Father's house?" *Why were we searching for you? You were a day away from being on the back of a milk carton, that's why, young man.*

They went looking for him once; thought in their minds that he might need psychiatric help (Mark 3:21, 31–35). Mary and family are so concerned that they interrupt one of his public lectures. "Hey Jesus, your mother and your brothers are outside looking for you; they're a little worried." Do you remember what Jesus said that day? Looking out at the crowd he says, "Who are my mother and brothers? Anyone who acts upon the word of God is my true family." Okay, I accept that. But how do you think Mary felt when that little nugget of theological wisdom got back to her later that day?

The truth, if you look at the Bible closely, is that every single instance where Jesus and his family are together in scripture seems to be fraught with heartache and worry inspired by Mary's son. So maybe Max Ernst is correct. Maybe Jesus needed an occasional spanking as a little boy. I'm not sure whether Mother's Day existed in the time of Jesus. But if the biblical evidence is any indicator, you have to wonder how Mary, mother of our Lord, may have spent her special day.

~

One of my favorite stories about early family life in the Bible comes from Numbers 12:1–16. Miriam and Aaron, siblings of Moses, are not happy with their famous brother. They sense that he's gotten a little too big for his britches. "Has the Lord spoken only through Moses? Has he not spoken through us also?" God heard the arguing and said, "Come out, you three, to the tent of meeting" (12:4). I have it on good authority that this gathering creatively foreshadows what we now call a "Come-to-Jesus meeting."

It's a tense time there in the tent. The Lord God is rather terse with Miriam and Aaron. He says how he typically speaks to visiting prophets through visions and dreams. But Moses is different. "With him I speak face to face—clearly, not in riddles" (12:8). The meeting ends abruptly. For the perceived impertinence against her brother, Miriam is struck with leprosy and cast out of the camp for seven days, despite Moses's failed prayer of healing for his sassy sister.

I have to wonder if there was some of this tension in Jesus's family among his own siblings as our Lord's stature and reputation grew. We get just a hint of this in the prologue to John's gospel: "He was in the world, and the world came into being through him; yet the world did not know him. He came to what was his own, and his own people did not accept him" (1:10–11). I cannot imagine what it would be like to be found unacceptable by your own people.

There is a striking detail about family dynamics in the old story of "the man born blind" in John 9:1–41. At one point, after repeated questions voiced by the religious authorities, the parents of this healed man are hauled downtown to explain their son's good fortune. The room heats up. Mom and dad start to squirm a little. They basically wash their hands of the matter and refuse to defend their son. "Ask him; he is of age. He will speak for himself" (9:21). I'm curious whether this old story reveals more biographical detail from Jesus's own home life than we might guess.

≈

I figure that if God created the world and created hippopotami and trillium and giraffes and the Milky Way and over fifty galaxies for each of the six billion people on the planet, then God can probably manage a pregnancy that does not follow the regular traffic patterns. *How* it happened is not really the question for me anymore. I'm much more intrigued about the impact this baby had on his own household, his parents and siblings, as he grew in wisdom and stature. We don't have a lot of hard evidence about this home life, but what we do have is enough to make a few guesses.

At "The Cloisters" just outside of New York City, there is a famous painting of the Annunciation. Gabriel is talking to Mary. Slipping down a shaft of sunlight towards Mary is the embryonic Jesus. Look closely and you will notice that he is already carrying his cross. The behavior of Mary before and just after the birth of Jesus—ponderous, patient, magnifying the Lord—quietly foreshadows the cross that will await her child. She was his mom, but in many ways she was also his first disciple, suggesting the shape of the Christian household.

When Mary said "yes" to Gabriel and to God, she began to carry a cross. She placed God's call ahead of what would have been a very safe and predictable life. *She agreed to carry Jesus with her.* "Let it be with me according to your word" (Luke 1:38). Let it be. Those words would give birth to a famous Beatles song centuries later, of course. But when they were first uttered, the words cost the speaker a great deal—her reputation, undoubtedly, as an unwed teenage mother, but also any semblance of a normal family life. She was mom in a very strange, exciting, and unpredictable household. Mary's sacrificial behavior reveals the nature of any faithful Christian home.

"The Holy Spirit will come upon you, and the power of the Most High will overshadow you" (Luke 1:35). *The Holy Spirit will come upon you.* This, of course, is exactly what occurs during every baptism in every congregation across the world. When you were conceived as a Christian, when baptismal water broke at a marvelous and wondrous birth, the Holy Spirit came upon *you.* The Most High overshadowed *you.* You were born into a new family, the household of God.

Ponder that.

3

Jesus and the American Family[1]

Memory and imagination seem to me the same human property, known by different names. Clark Kent and Superman are, after all, the same muscular guy; the only difference between them lies in how they are packaged and perceived.[2]

—Tony Earley

Maybe it was setting the ditch on fire with gasoline for no apparent reason, just to see what it would look like. Maybe it was the pair of sharp scissors thrown into my brother's bedroom door, coming to rest with a resounding *thwock*. Maybe it was the time my older brother knocked me out cold just outside Cawood's Barber Shop, the barber looking down at me in the alley, ready to call for help or maybe smelling salts. Maybe it was when I backed my little brother up against the wall in the carport and made him spread arms and legs like they do in the circus, surrounding him with a neat geometric pattern of darts until an errant throw stuck in his leg. (The little pansy never cried until my father got home.) Maybe it was the coffee table we came near smashing in a wrestling

1. Portions of this next section, in slightly different form, first appeared in Honeycutt, "Eventual Grace," 12–13.

2. Earley, *Somehow Form a Family*, xviii.

match that got out of hand, my mother pushing us out the door in a tangled heap to save the furniture. Or maybe it was how my younger brother went to work for the George McGovern campaign at age fourteen in downtown Chattanooga and my older brother became one of Jesse Helms's greatest fans when he moved to North Carolina. Family beach reunions are still rather fascinating.

Maybe it's all of these things reminding me that growing up with brothers can be sort of hormonally tense and that nothing we read in Genesis about those two ancient brothers, Jacob and Esau, should surprise us. Some people new to the Bible are rather shocked about the first book of the Holy Scriptures because there you will find the whole menu of human folly and flawed behavior in one tidy little volume—murder, betrayal, infidelity, lying, cheating, megalomania, revenge, it's all there. You'd think such a big black bestseller like the Bible would open with a nice soufflé of general principles; sweet rules to live by. But no; just a couple chapters in and we bump into fratricide. Hey, my brothers and I only threw scissors.

The Bible has staying power over the millennia not because it describes valorous people who have summoned their very best behavior to overcome life's obstacles in admirable ways. Not even close. The Bible is our book not because it tells the story of perfect people and how you better become one or else. The Bible is our book because it tells the story of how God looks at the world and sees a mess and chooses to love us in spite of such. In other words, the Bible is our book because we see the details of our fallen lives all over its pages and God works with us anyway.

So imagine with me a brother camped all alone beside an old river. Why is he alone? Well, because he is afraid. He has just moved his entire family—fifteen people, eleven of them children—across the river in the middle of the night (Gen 32:22–23). When I was hiking the Appalachian Trail many years ago, there was a very difficult ford of the Kennebec River in Maine. Today they ferry you across for free in a canoe, but back then you walked with all your gear in swift river depths that came up to mid-thigh. Water was released upstream at times that made the river even deeper; there were lots of unsteady stones underfoot. I was glad to get across.

I recently went online and looked up a picture of the Jabbok River—not as formidable as the Kennebec, I'll admit, but still quite a challenge for Jacob's family after dark. It seems like a nutty thing to do after the sun has gone down, to cross any river with eleven children—the sort of thing that would get the Department of Social Services' investigative juices flowing. That accomplished, Jacob then beds down on the opposite shore and watches the campfire of his family slowly go out.

Read a little earlier in Genesis 32 and discover why Jacob is behaving irrationally. Jacob's brother, Esau, is heading his way with 400 men. My brother may have knocked me out once in a front of a barber shop but he never threatened to kill me. Twenty years prior, Jacob cheated Esau out of birthright and blessing. Jacob duped his old father whose sight was waning. Jacob's mother assisted in the ruse of putting one over on the old man. "Ha-ha, we can fool the blind idiot." Dysfunctional families are nothing new. Sometimes when I think the Honeycutt family has problems, I'll just pick up the Book of Genesis and read around a bit. Without fail, I always feel better. Perspective is a very underrated gift.

So Jacob is camped there, by the river; alone. He's already prayed the foxhole prayer to God: "Deliver me please, from the hand of my brother, for I am afraid of him. He may come and kill us all" (Gen 32:11). Ever the shrewd one, Jacob has already sent ahead a virtual Noah's Ark of animals as a gift for his brother—a menagerie of goats, sheep, camels, cows, and donkeys; 540 animals by my count in various waves. I can only imagine Esau's stunned reaction as the animals showed up. It was like The Heifer Project catalog coming alive and landing in his camp.

And so after all the presents, after the foxhole prayer, and after sending his family across the river, an anxious Jacob finally lies down to sleep. You'd think this guy who had dreams with a stone as a pillow could sleep through anything. But sleep does not come. A reunion is about to occur. If your last high school reunion brought any stress, ratchet up Jacob's reunion anxiety several notches as he tries to pray, "Now I lay me down to sleep."

In the year 1659, the great Dutch artist Rembrandt painted this old Bible scene of Jacob wrestling. I usually love Rembrandt, but in this case I think he gets the story badly wrong. In the painting, the angel who wrestles with Jacob seems to be almost gently embracing him. Jacob's eyes are closed, his head resting on the angel's shoulder. There is such sympathy oozing from the eyes of the divine visitor. The angel seems to be saying, "You've been through so much. There, there now." No, sorry, Rembrandt. I see sweat in this old wrestling match. I see grunting and shouting. I see an old cheater (that is what Jacob's name means) coming to terms with his past. I see Jacob walking with a limp after receiving a new name.

This is a scene where we learn that God takes our past seriously so that he can create a whole new future, a whole new family. Sometimes the whole process will leave us limping. Esau and Jacob do reconcile after twenty years of enmity. Esau runs (33:4) across the field to hug his wayward brother in an action that foreshadows the parable of the Prodigal Son.

Jacob wrestled beside a river. He wrestled with his past. He wrestled with God. It was almost like labor. And something new was born. We also wrestle with our past beside an old river. The source of this river flows through countless fonts. It's an old story. In baptism we also are given a new name—child of God; the promise of a new family born out of many a checkered past.

≈

For several years I've saved an article from *The New Yorker* concerning the booming Bible business in the United States. "Research has found that ninety-one percent of American households own at least one Bible—the average household owns four—which means that Bible publishers manage to sell twenty-five million copies a year of a book that almost everybody already has."[3] Despite

3. Radosh, "The Good Book Business," 54.

skyrocketing sales each year, theologian William Stringfellow once prophetically (and ironically) noted: "The weirdest corruption of contemporary American Protestantism is its virtual abandonment of the Word of God in the Bible."[4] Do American Christians own several copies of a revered book we rarely read? I used to think that Christians didn't read the Bible because they were too busy. I've since decided, after over a quarter-century as a parish pastor, that biblical illiteracy among people of faith is attributable more to the difficult change demanded by the church's book when we actually open it. When Lutheran church council leaders of my past acquaintance have a hard time explaining how Galatians differs from Lamentations (or locating these respective books within the Bible itself), the church (and congregational families therein) has a problem.

I've always appreciated the honesty of the good folk who "begged Jesus to leave their neighborhood" (Matt 8:34) after the healing of two demoniacs and the drowning of local swine. Perhaps they were piqued at economic loss. But maybe they mirror our own twenty-first century feelings about Jesus: it's important to have him on the shelf just in case, but a little of the man's teachings can go a long way. Isn't life easier without Jesus? One of the most popular YouTube installments of 2012 ("Facebook Parenting: For the Troubled Teen") reveals an angry father, also a follower of Jesus, who calls out his ungrateful and undisciplined daughter online by taking her laptop to his back pasture and filling it with bullet holes. The video had 36 million hits (as of December 2012) and hundreds of comments from supportive parents. We're never told whether this got the daughter's attention, but the message is clear: a father's violent ire trumps anything Jesus might have to say on the subject.

Americans often choose to sugarcoat the Bible's inherent "holiness" (it says so right there on the spine) with hundreds of choices for every niche group imaginable:

4. Kellerman, ed., *A Keeper of the Word*, 167.

> There are devotional Bibles for new believers, couples, brides, and cowboys. On an airplane recently, I saw a woman reading a surfers' Bible . . . The variety is seemingly limitless. Nelson Bible Group's 2006 catalogue lists more than a hundred titles.[5]

Such a wide variety of choices suggests a personal need for scripture to tangentially support a chosen lifestyle shaped by a variety of cultural forces rather than a life formed by the wider message of the Bible itself.

I received a phone call just after the shootings in Newtown, Connecticut, from a concerned mother in our community. Her son had "a really great idea" to help the elementary school children who died in the tragedy. "He wants to inflate hundreds of helium balloons, every color in the rainbow, and send them to heaven on Christmas Eve" so the children can enjoy them "up there." Could I make an appeal to the congregation (a dollar per member) asking for their help with this project? I listened patiently, but wound up telling her we had many children to help on the ground. She did not like this answer, of course. I was reminded in this exchange of God's answer to Job as they debated the mysteries of suffering and the profundities of creation, including the unbridled Leviathan: "Will you play with it as with a bird, or will you put it on a leash for your girls?" (Job 41:5). It's just not possible to put a smiley-face on every unexplainable event in the world. Without the gift of scripture, Christians resort to banalities that try to make suffering go down easier. We cannot tie a balloon to the cross. I think we know this deep down, but Christian families often "consult the ghosts and the familiar spirits that chirp and mutter" (Isa 8:19) because at least there's some noise; it seems so much more comforting than silence, even though Job (2:13) clearly prefers such during his troubles instead of the "helpful" comments of his chatty friends.

5. Radosh, "The Good Book Business," 54–55.

Fresh out of seminary, I recall sitting with young couples in my office for their (organ music here) PRE-MARITAL COUNSELING sessions. If they wanted to be married in the church, they had to get by me first, by golly, the ecclesiastical gatekeeper. And they had to understand the nature of their commitment to each other and to God. With marriages crumbling all around me, I took these sessions with grave seriousness.

Conversely, however, the couples generally did not. They would hold hands throughout the hour and maybe even kiss on cue and generally look at each other rather goofily. It's hard to counsel twenty-two-year-olds who are head over heels. It occasionally struck me as we sat there that I was intruding on their adoration for one another and that I should perhaps leave the room, or maybe get them a room. I felt somewhat like a pastoral policeman shining a flashlight onto their backseat bliss—an unwanted prowler, a theological voyeur. Enraptured with each other, they usually tolerated my questions.

"Well, why do you want to get married?" I used to ask them. Wiser now, I never ask this anymore. Couples looked at me as if I'd stepped off another planet. Their eyes searched mine as if to say, "Well, isn't it obvious, Einstein?" One couple told me there were plenty of wedding chapels in Gatlinburg and they sure didn't need this. I pressed onward, the relentless interrupter. And they said, every couple, as if on cue, "Well, we *love* each other." But usually, the word came out *luuuvv*, almost dripping off the tongue. "We *luuuvv* each other, pastor. Forever."

I don't have anything against the heart going pitty-patter, cupid frolicking with his arrow, or even the word "love" intoned as if one is pouring syrup. But I have come to know that it has relatively little to do with a healthy relationship. *Relatively* little. And a whole lot to do with a high divorce rate.

In our culture, love is primarily defined as a feeling, an emotion; a sentiment. I'm not saying this is wrong. I am saying it predominates. And if you really *luuuvv* somebody, your romantic feelings for them will be constant and true and the same yesterday, today, and forever. I truly think that most divorces, certainly not all, are related to this glassy-eyed notion of what it means to love another person. Pastor Tim Suttle describes how sentimentality affects church life:

> Sentimentality is mother's milk to the church which has ceased to believe our faith should really make a difference in the way we live our lives. Instead of proclaiming resurrection, the sentimental church will devote their entire Sunday worship service to Mother's/Father's Day—or worse yet, Valentine's Day. Not that we don't appreciate our parents and sweethearts, but the yielding of precious worship time to the celebration of greeting card companies signals a much deeper problem: we have lost track of the story of God. Yet, for a church to grow bigger, losing track of the story is precisely what is required. Instead of pursuing faithfulness the sentimental church must provide a place where people can come to hear a comforting message from an effusive pastor spouting fervent one-liners which are intended only to make us feel good about the decisions we've already made with our lives.[6]

In the Bible love is primarily *not* an emotion. There are romantic, even erotic, examples of love in the scriptures, but love in the Bible is primarily a *practice* and not a feeling. Jesus says, "This is my commandment, that you love one another as I have loved you. No one has greater love than this, to lay down one's life for one's friends" (John 15:12–13).

Please notice two central things about Jesus's words here. First, this is a commandment. Jesus doesn't say, "Hey, here's a little suggestion you can accept or ignore." Jesus never says, "Think about loving this way, won't you? Please consider it." No, it's *commanded.* This is not Multiple Choice, an option to ponder when I happen to get around to it or a way of life when I feel so inclined. These are marching orders. This is tough for us in a land

6. Suttle, "How to Shrink Your Church."

of freedom—nobody telling me what to do! "Obedience" is not a word we readily embrace. It makes us nervous when Jesus says things like, "I chose you, you did not choose me." Where is our cherished freedom in the matter?

Here's a line that gets uttered with increasing frequency in our culture: "You know, I just don't feel like going to church today. Just don't feel like it." Who hasn't felt or said that? Even pastors sometimes say it! I have learned, over time, to be distrustful of many of my feelings. I realize that culturally my last sentence is almost akin to saying, "Let's burn the American flag today." We've been taught that feelings are everything. "Trust your feelings, Luke," recalls the famous line from *Star Wars*. "Trust your feelings." To tell you the truth, I've learned that mine are often untrustworthy.

Perhaps Jesus knew that feelings often follow action and not the other way around. If I waited until I "felt" like it, I'd often be waiting quite a long time. I'm convinced that only on rare occasions do we feel our way into action. In fact, the converse is usually true: *we act our way into feelings*. This is true in relationships, in church life, and life in general. If you're wondering why Jesus listed love as a "commandment," this is probably the reason.

We are commanded to love not just any old way, but to love "as" Jesus loved. That's a devastating little word—"as." Two letters; lots of implications. Someone said that disciples should be prepared to look good on wood. Love looks more like a cross than a heart-shaped Valentine. And yet there's not really a market at Hallmark for Good Friday cards, have you noticed? But every healthy relationship, friendship, or discipleship will have sacrificial love at its center. A relationship that lacks a cross-like love is essentially over. This is as true of marriage and family as it is of church life. In the movie *Shenandoah*, Jimmy Stewart is a farmer and a recent widower, somewhat cynical, who prays the following table prayer with his sons: "Lord, we cleared this land. We plowed it, sowed it, and harvested it. We cooked the harvest. It wouldn't be here and we wouldn't be eatin' it if we hadn't done it all ourselves. We worked dog-bone hard for every crumb and morsel. But we thank you just the same for this food we're about to eat. Amen." Without

Christ at the center of family life, everything boils down to our own best efforts.

≈

"This is my commandment, that you love one another *as* I have loved you." I wonder what would happen if congregations slowed down and seriously pondered this single verse for a whole year. What would happen to the health of our marriages and families; what would happen in our workplaces, in our neighborhoods, with our financial and service commitments? One verse; fourteen words, for a whole year.

We need to stop swallowing the lie that *luuuvv* will keep us all together. We are saved (saved from ourselves to tell you the truth) by a different love. The reckless, life-giving, cross-shaped salvation of Jesus.

When we get that straight, well, that's what the Bible calls church.

4

Jesus and the New Family

Since no one can possibly read the whole Bible, what we do instead is create our own Bible-within-a-Bible, where we focus on the important parts—like why we're not going to Hell, despite our constant stream of lustful thoughts and visceral dislike of beggars—and forget the unimportant parts, like those obscure passages about rich people being in trouble. This is perfectly natural and normal, and in fact, Christians have been doing it since early days, which is why you rarely see the Epistle of Titus cited by anyone outside Titus' immediate family.[1]

—FROM *THE MESSIAH FORMERLY KNOWN AS JESUS*

He saw the heavens torn apart and the Spirit descending like a dove on him . . . and the Spirit immediately drove him out into the wilderness.

—MARK 1:10, 12

PART ONE: Okay, now let me get this straight. God got mad once and flooded the earth. I realize that it's debatable how one reads this story, but let's go with the details as presented in the Bible. God got angry, sent more water than Katrina or Sandy (or name

1. Breen, *The Messiah Formerly Known as Jesus*, 62.

your hurricane) could shake a stick at, and drowned all the people except for a single faithful family. Forty days go by. Noah sends out a dove to test whether there's any place to dock the boat and on the third try the dove does not return.

The fortunate family and their mooing, squealing, bleating entourage find a safe, habitable port and begin to repopulate the earth. (Lots of crazy racial repopulation theories exist, of course, tracing all human ancestry back to this watery escape, but that's another discussion for another day.) Am I getting the details fairly right? Onward then.

Maybe I'm missing something here, but it seems like God is a bit ashamed of himself for drowning all those people. Three times God says, "Never again." Three times. God is through with such attention-getting devices like floods and maybe begins to wonder if they really work in the first place. So a covenant is drafted between God and "all flesh" to help put people at ease the next time thunder clouds gather on the horizon.

God hangs his "bow" in the clouds; a colorful rainbow promise, yes, but also a wordplay that God will not resort to such violence ever again. His bow (as in "bow and arrow") has been retired in the sky. It's been hung up and will "never again" be used.

But this covenant, this promise, is rather odd, don't you think? God says, "When the bow is in the clouds, I will see it and remember the everlasting covenant between God and every living creature on the earth" (Gen 9:16). I like the idea, but doesn't it surprise you that God needs a little reminder—a celestial "sticky-note" in the sky, a divine "string around the finger" of sorts, a multi-colored wake-up call? "When I see the rainbow," God says, "my memory will be jogged never to do this flood thing again." It's all right there in the story. We tend to edit out the strange details of Noah's famous ark when we tell it to children, or paint the scene on nursery bedroom walls with giraffes and bunnies hopping out of the boat.

I'm going to fast-forward several Bible centuries now, but before doing so, please ponder this question: *When Noah released that dove the third time, never to return, where did that bird of peace go?*

PART TWO: Jesus is standing in a river, up to his waist in water—at least that deep. The heavens are torn apart. A resonant voice rumbles across the sky. One detail of this baptism that we like to remember is that a dove swoops down and lands on our Lord's head. Are we supposed to remember that other dove, the one released from the ark so long ago? Maybe so. "Never again," said God. "Never again will I act in such a way."

As Jesus stands in that river, the heavens are torn apart, the sky rumbles just a bit, and I'll admit that no rain is falling on anybody's head. But there is something else afoot here. God does not send a flood to the earth, but he sure seems to send Jesus into one. "And the Spirit [which came to Jesus in the guise of that dove] immediately drove him out into the wilderness" (Mark 1:12). The dove drove him. Just a single letter separates those two words—words we don't normally associate with each other.

It's a fairly strong word to describe the action of the Holy Spirit. I like other words—coax, coddle, plead, encourage. That's the Spirit we're used to. Do you know this song? *Spirit, Spirit of gentleness, blow through the wilderness, calling and free*. I like that hymn but this is no "gentle" spirit depicted here. This bird turns into a hawk and "drives" Jesus (moments after his bath) into the wilderness to do business with the devil for forty days. Wait a minute. Wasn't that the length of time Noah and family were on that ark? The dove departs the boat and lands several centuries later on the head of Jesus. Now I know it's not the same dove, but there's enough symbolism here to drown a poet. Not a single Bible verse in Mark's Gospel separates the baptism of Jesus and his encounter with Satan and "the wild beasts." He is *driven* into the desert by that dove.

PART THREE: "Now look at little Jimmy, would you? He's about to get a little water poured over his sweet little head. It's his baptism day. Isn't he a sweet little boy? Smile for the camera everybody and then please join us for a little cake and punch afterwards."

It's hard for us to think very long about what's actually at stake in baptism. We often sugarcoat the sacrament, but the Bible uses very different language. In the Bible, God promises to never send another flood, but he makes no such promise about sending Jesus into the metaphorical equivalent. And if you think about it, there's no such promise to us: the latter-day baptized. We face similar temptations; we live with similar "wild beasts" (Mark 1:13) that Jesus encountered. Baptism does not inoculate God's people from pain and suffering.

I occasionally receive a phone call from a worried stranger who says in a panic, "Will you do my baby?" After a second or two passes, I realize they're asking for baptism. They want some sort of holy reassurance that nothing will ever befall their child. According to this story, baptism does not protect us from evil. In fact, it may heighten and quicken our encounter with such. Jesus gets wet (and hardly dries off) before the devil comes knocking.

PART FOUR: So let me make sure I've got this right. The dove leaves the boat; the ark finds dry land. "Never again," says God. "No more floods." I like to think of that dove flying across the centuries; finally finding rest, a port, in the person of Jesus. He is our New Ark, Lord of the church. In him we find safety, harbor, and purpose.

But similar to Jesus's baptism, ours is not a sweet little splash into the next life. We are set apart in baptism to do battle with the beasts, both real and figurative, of this world. As Luther puts it in his famous hymn: "In battle we'll engage." The promise of baptism is not to protect us from the flood, but to give us courage to engage the waters that sometimes swallow and drown people. There is One who has been there before us. He is Lord of all, victorious over evil—captain of this New Ark, this new family named church that survives the rage of any storm.

≈

Slowly, he eased me backwards. When the water closed over the top of me I did not shut my eyes, and in the instant he held me there I could see the world above me as if through a sheet of uneven glass—the gray rim of sky, the small brown faces crowded around, the warped, faraway form of Elder Turley. I lay back, suspended in that perfect moment before I was lifted up with one great rushing pull and I broke the surface, blinking and sputtering and weightless, made of nothing but air.[2]

—FROM *THE MIRACLE LIFE OF EDGAR MINT*

But when the fullness of time had come, God sent his Son, born of a woman, born under the law, in order to redeem those who were under the law, so that we might receive adoption as children.

—GALATIANS 4:4–5

"Whoever comes to me and does not hate father and mother, wife and children, brothers and sisters, yes, and even life itself, cannot be my disciple."

—LUKE 14:26

"For I have come to set a man against his father, and a daughter against her mother . . . Whoever loves father or mother more than me is not worthy of me; and whoever loves son or daughter more than me is not worthy of me."

—MATTHEW 10:35A, 37

He himself is before all things, and in him all things hold together. He is the head of the body, the church; he is the beginning, the firstborn from the dead, so that he might come to have first place in everything.

—COLOSSIANS 1:17–18

2. Udall, *The Miracle Life of Edgar Mint*, 236.

Dear Dad,[3]

Well, Happy Father's Day to you. If I'm counting correctly, this is your fiftieth Dad's Day, a half-century of paternal wisdom passed down. Beginning in April in the mid-1950s, your three boys came along like clockwork in almost exact two-year intervals (you've always had impeccable timing). Three sons made you the Fred McMurray of East Brainerd in Chattanooga.

Thanks for all the time you spent with me as a child—for teaching me how to throw a baseball and how to run a convincing "buttonhook." For explaining the fine art of the "bump and run" chip shot with a seven iron and how to catch a wave just so at the beach, not too early or late. For shooting all those baskets in the driveway and playing "H-O-R-S-E" until the floodlights came on. For forgiving me when I wrecked the car. For the honest "sex talk" in the living room so long ago, even though I was shy and didn't really want to talk about it.

Our home was a safe place to grow up. And I don't want to be overly romantic here and pretend that ours was a family free from problems or my parents were without flaws. You've been a Lutheran Christian all your life and know what a lie that would be. But you and mom provided me a place to grow and discover and even learn from failing. And for that I am truly thankful.

But here's the thing. Have you ever noticed this? As a nation is rightfully grateful each June for the sacrifices of dads across the land, you may recall that Jesus in the Bible says, oddly: "Don't think that I've come to bring peace to the earth. I haven't come to bring peace, but rather a sword. For I have come to set a man against his father, and a daughter against her mother" (Matt 10:34–35). When you and mom brought me forward for baptism on that hot July Sunday back in 1957, did you know that Jesus sometimes appears to speak like a crazy man? When Pastor Cadwallader poured water over my bald baby head at Ascension Lutheran downtown and handed me back to you that summer so long ago, announcing

3. The following letter first appeared (in slightly different form) in Honeycutt, "Our 50 Father's Days."

that my Christian life had just begun, did you know that nothing would ever be the same again?

"I have come to set a man against his father," says Jesus. Sometimes I wonder why Jesus talked this way to his disciples—what he could have *possibly* meant. And I wonder why people just don't run the other way from this man; if they really know what's at stake when they bring their little ones forward for this ancient sacrament of washing and welcome. I recall another passage where Saint Paul asks with some urgency: "Do you not know that when you were baptized into Jesus Christ you were baptized into his death? Therefore we have been buried with him by baptism into death" (Rom 6:3–4). *Happy Baptism Day, little one. We've just drowned and raised you in the waters.* In baptism, I have died. You have died already, both of us swimming around in the grace of God ever since.

Did you and mom know all this when you brought me forward on that summer Sunday so long ago? Did I know it when I brought my own son and daughters? That we literally *die* in these waters? Raised to a new life in a new family that scrambles old allegiances and traditional family loyalties? Did you know that the name of Honeycutt and the family love we had for each other at 6939 Hickory View Lane would not be enough to sustain us in this life? That you were bringing me forward for a crucifixion of sorts?

And see, I think you did know; you must have known. You knew that fallible, flawed earthly dads, no matter how much time or attention they pay to their children, can never muster the kind of love that God's children need to thrive. In fact, I suppose it's possible to love a child so much that we smother them, suffocate them.

And so this is what I thank you for the most on this Father's Day—that you loved me enough to introduce me to a greater love, a surpassing love: the love of the eternal Father whose family reaches across time and space with a long genealogy linked not by last name, but by water and word. You encouraged an allegiance that was greater than our little family—knowing, I suspect, your own limits and frailties, as I've certainly come to know mine in my own household here in South Carolina.

I'm thinking of you today, dad, and all those games of H-O-R-S-E, and all those tight spirals you threw in the backyard until darkness fell. But here as we all grow older, and shadows lengthen in all of our lives, I'm recalling this seemingly odd man you introduced me to by bringing me to church Sunday after Sunday. "I have come to set a man against his Father," he said. When you brought me for baptism, did you really know that Jesus would demand this radical shift in allegiance?

I think you did. You knew that it was only with Jesus's help that any of us could be a better father, a better parent, a better son, a better friend. On this special day, I thank you for spending so much time with me. And I thank you for loving me. But I thank you most of all for leading me to a greater love, a wider family, a blessed lineage where water is even thicker than blood.

Happy Father's Day, Dad . . .

Your son, Frank

≈

In September of 1985 our first child was born. We named her Hannah, which means "grace." Later that fall (October 20th to be precise) we placed her up for adoption. A pastor poured water over her head in church one Sunday and said something like, "Once you were just a Honeycutt, but now you're adopted into a much larger family—the family of God that stretches with a strange genealogy further than you can possibly see. These odd ones are your kin now. You'll be sent to unusual places one day. Welcome."

Several years passed. Cindy and I were sitting around the kitchen table. Hannah played with the black cat at our feet. (Every minister needs a black cat.) We'd been praying, asking God to guide and help us as we made decisions about a second child. We heard about a little girl in an orphanage in El Salvador as war raged around the countryside there. Cindy scheduled a flight with the only ticket we could afford. With a set of details that could only have been orchestrated by the Holy Spirit, we adopted Marta in December of 1988. Exactly a month later we placed her up for adoption again. The pastor said something like, "Once you were a Salvadoran, and then just a Honeycutt, but now you're adopted into a much larger family—the family of God that stretches further than you can possibly see. These odd ones are your kin now. You'll be sent to unusual places one day. Welcome."

I was bicycling one May on the Blue Ridge Parkway with my cycling pals on our annual week-long trip. It was before the advent of cell phones. A ranger stopped me on a long climb. I was glad to stop, winded, but thought someone back home had died. "Are you Frank Honeycutt?" asked the ranger. I nodded yes. "Your wife wants you to call her." I rode to the nearest telephone. It all came at once. "The mother cannot keep the little boy. He's biracial—black father, white mother. It's a very small town. We need to make a decision in the next week. She's in her last trimester." We drove to Tennessee, a small town near Nashville, in early July of 1991 and picked Lukas up at the hospital. He was four days old at the time of his adoption. A little over a month later we placed him up for adoption again. The pastor in church that Sunday said something like, "Many people will want to define you by your race or by your last name, but now by water and the word you're adopted into a much larger family—the family of God. These odd ones are your kin now. And you'll be sent to unusual places one day. Welcome."

Several Christmases ago we were watching a movie in our den downstairs when I heard Marta's voice upstairs in the kitchen. "Dad, could you come up here and see something please?" Parked comfortably on the sofa, I urged her to bring it to me. "I can't, Dad," she pleaded. "Please come." There in the kitchen, looking terrified, a little girl was standing in a puddle of red Kool-Aid that covered every floor tile in the room. She looked at me, and then the floor; back and forth repeatedly—waiting for my reaction, maybe my wrath. She had dropped what we repeatedly told her was too heavy to begin with; guilty, poised in a sticky purgatory, waiting for a verdict.

How do we learn to live together in a family? We look to one who will hang with arms outstretched in the middle of another red pool collecting at his feet, mercifully erasing the messy and sticky charges against us in the here and now. God welcomes us in baptism into a new family of grace. "Father forgive them, they don't know what they're doing" (Luke 23:34). Without Jesus in the very center of family life, households may resort to a hundred different unhealthy possibilities for solving the messes we find ourselves in. With Jesus the promises of how to live together are endless: "We are afflicted in every way, but not crushed; perplexed, but not driven to despair; persecuted, but not forsaken; struck down, but not destroyed; always carrying in the body the death of Jesus, so that the life of Jesus may also be made visible in our bodies" (2 Cor 4:8–10). God adopts us in baptism into an unusual family where forgiveness always has the last word.

~

Sometimes I wonder if Jesus might have benefited from an advisor or two. I hope that doesn't sound blasphemous to tender ears, but really now. *What is Jesus thinking in these strange teachings about the family?*

"Large crowds were traveling with Jesus" (Luke 14:25). Maybe he's at the equivalent of the Galilee State Fair. Flocks of admirers surround him. The polls are up for the Lord, in other words. He's a popular guy and people hang on every word. That's a sure sign of success in politics or sports or church life, correct? If the crowds are present, then things must be going well.

I was at the Florida State-Clemson game a couple years ago, my first visit back to my alma mater for a football game since the fall of 1978. Eighty-three thousand orange-clad fanatics packed into Death Valley. I got kind of misty-eyed when the team ran down the hill, touched Howard's Rock, and the band broke into the Tiger Rag. But what if only 500 people had shown up in that spacious place? We'd have to conclude that something was terribly wrong among the Tiger Nation. The same is true in church life. We very often measure success through numbers—two numbers in particular: church attendance and offering dollars. When those are down, we wring our collective hands and wonder what we're doing wrong.

Jesus is not too concerned about public opinion. He doesn't seem to have speech writers or appealing commercials claiming that discipleship will "solve all your problems." Jesus seems to have missed the course on image projection. Conventional wisdom assumes that he'd want these large crowds to get even larger. Jesus, however, says a few things that probably thinned out the throng considerably by the end of the day. Twenty centuries removed, I'm cringing for the guy and almost wish the disciples had carried some sort of ten-second delay device.

"Whoever comes to me and does not hate father and mother and family and, yes, even life itself, cannot be my disciple." Jesus said these offensive things at the *very zenith* of his popularity. "Large crowds" were hanging on his every word—maybe not 83,000 but enough to pay the bills and fund the movement and get this new thing called the kingdom of God up and running. Jesus would never have to rely again on a little boy's little lunch of fish and bread to feed everybody. The disciples could just collect a free-will offering and have the thing catered.

One of the reasons I love Jesus is that he refuses to play games in order to further his popularity. He demands a practical priority in our lives, even surpassing the commitment to those in our family. He knows that we can suffocate one another in the name of love. He knows that we can be no real good to family members unless we love them with the love and wisdom of Jesus rather than with our own best efforts. He knows that even the gift of family can become an idol. (By the way, don't let the word "hate" trip you up here. It's not the same as saying the venomous, "I hate you." It's a word denoting priority; primary allegiance.)

~

"Jesus is such a nice guy. Loves kids. Befriended the down and out. Gentle, meek, and mild; never got angry, never got mad at anybody. Just a great guy. He loves everybody. Forgives everything. Understands me like nobody else. Praise Jesus. Praise the Lord."

Ever heard something like that? That Jesus is our wise, all-understanding holy man who forgives all our little idiosyncrasies (let's not call them sins) like a kind, loving grandpa in the sky who's about as threatening as a cup of warm tea.

An Inquirers' Class (of a sort) once gathered around Jesus. The class participants are interested in following the man so let's give them credit here. They've heard something about the traveling teacher and want to throw their hats into the movement. So let's watch Jesus here. Maybe we can learn a thing or two about how to welcome new church members. Maybe a couple of hints from Jesus about southern hospitality and how to prepare good Lutheran coffee and offer clear directions to the restrooms, that sort of thing. Nothing too heavy. We don't want to scare anybody away, do we? We want to learn from Jesus how to get these inquirers to *come back* and be a part of us, right? So, let's have a seat in this Inquirers' Class taught by Jesus. I'll sit in the back with you and we'll just watch how Jesus does it and the topics he covers. We're just observers in the class, taking notes. We're invisible, really. By my count, three students have signed up.

Inquirer number 1 raises his hand. An eager-beaver. "I will follow you wherever you go" (Luke 9:57). Gosh, I like that. I mean if I were teaching that class that's the sort of thing that would get my Lutheran pastor head-counting attention. This guy's ready to jump ahead to New Member Sunday and serve on the Property Committee on the very first day of class. Don't you like his passion? His eagerness to get involved? *Wherever you go*, says inquirer number 1. Heck, this guy's ready to serve as a synod assembly delegate even before he's read the resolutions.

So what in the world is Jesus doing when he brings up accommodations and lodging and foxes and birds and how animals have better homes than he has? In fact, he's basically saying that he sleeps with the homeless, "nowhere to lay his head" (Luke 9:58). He looks at that first inquirer and seems to say, "There? Will you join me there? You said you would follow wherever I go. Are you willing to make your home with me and place your true security in me and not a mortgage?" Don't worry. I have one. And I will keep mine. But this first topic in Inquirers' Class with Jesus forces me to examine the location of my true home. And as a disciple, it cannot be 225 Woodland Way. Jesus is my home, my shelter, my real security. And if that is true, it makes all sorts of sense to make the man my primary investment and to live where he lives; to bring my heart into his various places of residence.

Places like this one, a story from Africa:

> Just a little distance away, the figure of a woman was slumped against a bunch of banana trees. There was dried blood on her face. She must have collapsed there and died, but the baby was alive. It was in her lap, its little hands groping at its mother's bared breast. And it was looking right at Deo. He stared back at it for a long moment. The baby wasn't crying. "It must be wondering where it is," he thought. It must be terrified like him. But he couldn't help the baby. He couldn't even help himself.[4]

Too many babies die in this world while I'm worried about my home mortgage. Is it possible I'm limiting the places where Jesus chooses to lay his head? Forgetful of my true home?

A second hand went up in Inquirers' Class that day. See him waving up front there? Jesus has just invited him to follow. And he too is eager to sign on. He just wants to do one little thing, which is actually a pretty big thing: attend the funeral for his father. My goodness, isn't this a reasonable request? I suspect you could have heard a pin drop in class that day as Jesus responded to the man's need. This single verse still echoes across the centuries in all its utter strangeness: "Let the dead bury their own dead" (Luke 9:60). Jesus could have probably smacked the man and it would have been less shocking.

If you really want to clear out an Inquirers' Class in America, suggest somehow that Jesus has priority over momma and daddy. For that is what is really going on here, stated in a rather startling

4. Kidder, *Strength in What Remains*, 125–26.

way. Jesus was not against *honoring* mother and father. It's one of the commandments, of course. The issue is one of priority.

If my dad died today, of course I'd be in a car on the way to Chattanooga to help plan a funeral service. But if I love my dad *more* than Jesus, it won't do him (or me) any good. We learn how to love one another from Jesus. "Love one another," he says. How? *As I have loved you.* He doesn't say, "Love one another as Grandpa Honeycutt used to do it." Our love is often flawed, sentimental, and even smothering if left to our own devices. Love that matters looks like a cross: sacrificial, baptismal, including (but never limited to) blood kin.

Okay, we're still sitting in the back of the room, taking notes; pencils at the ready. There's a third inquirer down front who hasn't walked out. And let me quickly say that's one thing congregations serious about Jesus will have to come to terms with. People sometimes leave a congregation not because they *haven't* heard Jesus, but because they *have.* "Enter through the narrow gate," says Jesus elsewhere. "For the gate is wide and the road is easy that leads to destruction, and there are many who take it. For the gate is narrow and the road is hard that leads to life, and there are few who find it" (Matt 7:13–14).

Jesus teaches this strange, paradoxical way so that we might have life; real life. The church must never water down the life Jesus offers in the name of accessibility, or numbers games, or under the guise to help pay our bills. Too much is at stake—namely, the gospel that means to breathe life in all its fullness (and strangeness) into followers pledging allegiance to a new family.

So, do you see him? This third would-be follower down front in our Inquirers' Class? "I will follow you, Lord; but let me first say farewell to those at my home" (Luke 9:61). The operative word here, maybe the most important word in the whole lesson, is *first.* Again, Jesus is not against family relationships, but he wants to know *who is first.* Please be clear: Jesus wants to be first not so he can punch your ticket into heaven. *Jesus wants to be first so that he can help you.* Help you in your family life. Help you in your friendships. Help you in your job. Help you in an illness. Help you with that ornery neighbor you want to smack. Help you with a young person who is having trouble.

Please understand. Jesus will try to help you whether you place him first or fiftieth. The grace of Jesus is not contingent upon how we rank him in our lives. But practically speaking, Jesus will have a hard time getting to us if we place him fiftieth. And he will soon be fiftieth if he is not first.

It is important for a Christian to regularly examine one's ultimate priority in this life. When we name what is first out loud that is our god—"that to which we assign ultimate allegiance," said Martin Luther. Putting Jesus first resolves a lot of problems. Namely, it resolves *who is Lord*. I promise you this not to sound ominous, but because it's true: if you don't choose a Lord, another will choose you. And you'll find yourself bowing before its false demands.

There is a very important part of this old lesson that I haven't mentioned so far. It occurs just before the Inquirers' Class gets underway. James and John, two disciples, are furious that a certain village rejects the teachings of Jesus (Luke 9:51–56). They want to call fire down from heaven and consume the infidels, the little wretches. Maybe that will get their attention. Jesus will have none of this. He refuses to teach from a perspective of fear, threat, or manipulation. He just moves on.

It strikes me that in families today, we are facing something similar. We allow many different things to come before Jesus and his teachings—teachings that offer us life and health. Even though we may not openly reject Jesus in our households, in many instances it amounts to about the same thing. Jesus still refuses to call down fire, blast us with warning, or yell at us from the heavens. He may just move on. Waiting for us to join him on the road, in the ongoing Inquirers' Class where we are all students of the one who says, "Follow me."

≈

I suspect you've heard people say the following at funerals, especially funerals where the deceased person has been married for many years in a healthy relationship. There is a long receiving line at the church or funeral home and someone in the family leans down to hug the widow and says, "Don't worry, Aunt Sally, it won't be long until you see Uncle Jim again and then the two of you will be together forever." Aunt Sally smiles and cries and everyone nods in approval.

I remember hearing of an instance, however, where the hoped-for heavenly reunion worked exactly the opposite way. The marriage had not gone so well; there was emotional abuse off and on for many years. But the sentiment was the same from well-meaning people at the funeral. "Don't worry. It won't be long and then you'll be together forever." A few days later, the widow asked her pastor to drop by. They settled into the den and she asked, "I'm never going to get away from him, am I?"[5]

In Luke 20:27–40, some Sadducees corner Jesus with a question about the resurrection—specifically about marriage, the next life, and who will be joined together should someone experience multiple unions in this life. Sadducees were sort of the "old-guard" of Judaism. For most of Jewish history the concepts of heaven and hell simply did not exist. Look high and low in the Old Testament, and mention of any afterlife at all, pleasant or unpleasant, is exceedingly rare. Some modern Jews in the days of Jesus believed in some form of life after death, but not the Sadducees. They thought it was all theological hogwash.

But they did know their Bibles. This riddle posed to Jesus in Luke 20 is based on two old bits of scripture—one a teaching, the other a story—which these skeptical Sadducees probably had in mind. The teaching is from the book of Deuteronomy: "When brothers reside together, and one of them dies and has no son, the wife of the deceased shall not be married outside the family to a stranger. Her husband's brother shall go in to her, taking her in

5. I'm indebted to Barbara Brown Taylor for this illustration.

marriage, and performing the duty of a husband's brother to her." And what if the brother refuses this duty? "Then the brother's wife shall go up to him in the presence of the elders, pull his sandal off his foot, and spit in his face . . . Throughout Israel his family shall be known as 'the house of him whose sandal was pulled off.'"[6] The Word of the Lord.

The second bit of scripture that the Sadducees probably had in mind as they brought their riddle to Jesus most certainly comes from the entertaining but little-known Book of Tobit, considered apocryphal by Protestants. It's one of my all-time favorite Bible stories that will not be told in Sunday School. But that will not stop me here.

In this story, Tobias, the faithful son of the book's namesake, locates and falls in love with his kinswoman named Sarah. Sarah has experienced a long string of rotten luck with her past marriages. Each of her seven husbands has died on their wedding night just as their marriage was being consummated. "All died on the night when they went in to her" (Tob 7:11). It's a rather bizarre and titillating tale. There's more.

So certain that he will have an eighth dead son-in-law on his hands, old Raguel, Sarah's father (who is no doubt almost bankrupt from all these weddings), gets up in the middle of the night to dig a grave (8:9) just outside his daughter's bedroom window. Tired of community ridicule, he wants to dispose of the body under the cover of darkness and lower it from the window straight into the hole. But lo and behold, the newlyweds survive the night this time with the help of a malodorous fish liver (8:3) that repulses the pesky demon responsible for the seven deaths. Tobias, the new husband, literally prays to God for "safe sex" before they begin the honeymoon. It's a remarkable prayer: "Blessed are you, O God of our ancestors, and blessed is your name in all generations forever ... I am now taking this kinswoman of mine, not because of lust, but with sincerity. Grant that [Sarah] and I may find mercy and that we may grow old together" (8:5–7). They do, and they do. For Sarah, the eighth time around works like a charm. I'm convinced

6. See Deut 25:5–10.

that this odd story was well known by the Sadducees who came to trick Jesus that day.

In the Sadducees' version of the riddle to Jesus, however, the woman dies after seven husbands, which seems reasonable, actually, if you think about it. Seven husbands would exhaust just about anybody. My wife tells me that one just about does her in.

"So Jesus, old pal, in this resurrection you seem to believe in, whose wife will this woman be? Huh? Answer that one, Einstein." Flying elbows into ribs all around. You may recall that Jesus often likes to play around with his accusers, countering riddles with another riddle, but not here. Here Jesus answers the question as if it was truly asked in earnest. "Those who belong to this age marry and are given in marriage," he says, "but those who are considered worthy of a place in that age and in the resurrection from the dead neither marry nor are given in marriage" (Luke 20:34–35). The encounter ends rather tellingly: "No one dared to ask him another question" (20:40).

Though I must admit that I'm personally curious about the resurrection life, this story has a similar effect on me. I dare not ask him another question either. The Bible is shockingly spare when it comes to describing what the resurrection will be like. This is the only time that Jesus talks about the resurrection in any detail in the Gospels. We have Easter stories about Jesus in the garden with Mary, on a road with two disciples, and on the beach cooking breakfast, but there's really next to nothing about what resurrection will be like for us. And when Paul ventures to talk about it in his letters, the language is often quite veiled and mysterious. "So it is with the resurrection of the dead. What is sown is perishable, what is raised is imperishable. It is sown in dishonor, it is raised in glory. It is sown in weakness, it is raised in power. It is sown a physical body, it is raised a spiritual body."[7] Any questions?

Jesus simply doesn't offer a lot of details about what life after death will be like. What we hear in Luke 20 is just about it. So quite often, to fill the void, we will construct more. "Don't worry, Aunt Sally, it won't be long and then you'll be together with Uncle

7. See 1 Cor 15:35–58.

Jim forever." It is sometimes hard, understandably so, for faithful couples to come to terms with the part of the vow that says, "*Until death do us part.*" After all, if both sides of a committed relationship believe in eternal life, why should death be the end of the marriage? What does the parting now mean?

Curiously, the only real specific tidbit about heaven that we're given by Jesus is that our relationships on earth will change in heaven. "In the resurrection from the dead, people neither marry nor are given in marriage." But why? Because, says Jesus, we are "children of God, being children of the resurrection" (20:36).

In other words, our concept of family will be changed. There will somehow be *one family*. And we will all be children with one single Parent—God. Relationships as we now know them will no longer need to be. Jesus closes with a telling description of God: "For to him all of them are alive" (20:38). We will notice siblings and relationships in heaven we never knew we had.

Jesus said shockingly little about the subject of heaven. In some ways his answer to the riddle of the Sadducees is itself a riddle to our ears. His words may trouble Christian families more than bring comfort. But it behooves us to begin thinking about these heavenly relationships now—an existence where we are all children with a single parent; one family of God.

If this is the way it one day will be, it seems that such a coming reality might shape how we spend our days, our time, and our money now. How does this wider view of "family" affect our stewardship in this life?

"For to him all of them are alive." All of them.

5

Household Economics According to Jesus

Therefore I intend to keep on reminding you of these things, though you know them already and are established in the truth that has come to you. I think it right, as long as I am in this body, to refresh your memory.

—2 PETER 1:12–13

"You did not lie to us but to God!"

—ACTS 5:4

TO GLEAN EVEN A glimmer of understanding from the bizarre story of Ananias and Sapphira, a wealthy couple in the early church mentioned only in Acts 5, it's important to back up a bit and prowl around in Acts 4. "Now the whole group of those who believed were of one heart and soul, and no one claimed private ownership of any possessions, but everything they owned was held in common . . . There was not a needy person among them, for as many as owned lands or houses sold them and brought the proceeds of what was sold. They laid it at the apostles' feet, and it was distributed to each as any had need" (Acts 4:32, 33–34).

In that same fourth chapter, Barnabas sells a field and lays the money (all of it) at the feet of the apostles. He was eventually a companion with Saint Paul on his missionary journeys and presumably it was this downsizing of land holdings that gave Barnabas the freedom to hit the road for Jesus. This is a clear teaching in Acts. Possessions can possess us. Their upkeep and maintenance can lead us off the "fret-meter," preventing Christian households from maturity in discipleship. Giving possessions, money, or land *away* diffuses the collective power these holdings have over any Christian family just in terms of maintenance and time.

My parents are in their eighties now, still living in Chattanooga. Every time I visit, I notice how their possessions are shrinking; given away, labeled clearly for a friend or family member. They tell me they're "getting ready." I walked into my childhood bedroom a couple years ago and my old poster of Hank Aaron (I loved the man) was down and gone. My mom would never fess up, but I think Hank made it to the landfill. Okay, so I draw the line at Hank Aaron posters. But it's a wise thing to start thinking about—downsizing. All the stuff we carry around that we're not using that someone else could use.

So was this early socialism in the early church? No one claimed private ownership. Everything was held in common. It would seem so. A couple of Christians die in this strange story from Acts 5. Maybe their hearts were not in it 100 percent, but they were Christians. The husband, Ananias, is buried and the grave filled in even before his wife knows she's a widow. No time to don black. No hymns. No affirming homily. No prayers. (At least we're not told of such.) Peter confronts Ananias about his wealth and he falls down dead as a doornail. It's a fairly sobering stewardship campaign there in the early church.

Three hours pass. What do you think those early Christians were talking about between burial of husband and arrival of wife? The story gives a little clue: "Great fear seized all who heard of the death of Ananias." You think? Maybe fear and a rush on number two pencils to make sure the financial balances are correct at home and hearth.

The wife finally arrives. Sapphira (I love her name) walks in rather innocently, without a clue that her husband is subterranean. And Peter, rather coldly if you ask me, asks the poor woman a trick question. "That (um) . . . that land that y'all sold. Was it for, uh, such and such a price?" It's almost like poor Sapphira is on a cruel quiz show where the host and audience all know she's in a bind, but with no lifeline. Two numbers float around the room—the sale price of the property and their offering to the church—and the two numbers don't match up. The same feet of the same gravediggers that disposed of her husband also carry out Sapphira. She's buried beside her husband. How generous and kind. A second little mound of earth in plain view: a silent message to all who would gaze in that direction and remember the fall pledge drive.

Again, verse 11: "Great fear seized the whole church and all who heard of these things." It's the first time the word "church" is used in Luke-Acts. Thousands became disciples at Pentecost a few chapters prior. Do you think average attendance went down in church after this early stewardship campaign? Or up?

So, was the early church in Acts indeed committed to socialism? Is that what this old story is about? That Ananias and Sapphira held back some of the proceeds of a land transaction and paid the price?

I once heard of a Baptist Church in Texas that wanted to get serious about stewardship—biblically serious. Their theologian-in-residence that year, Stanley Hauerwas from Duke Divinity School, was asked to speak about financial stewardship and provide some practical tips for the congregation. Hauerwas is a wonderfully acerbic and honest fellow. "Here's a practical tip, since you've asked," he said. "Every fall from here on out, require everyone who wants to be (and remain) a member here to stand up and state out loud their name, vocation, and annual salary."

A few people on the church council looked confused. "What do you mean?" they asked Stanley. "You know exactly what I mean. 'I'm Sally Jones. I'm an accountant. And I make $73,000 dollars a year.' 'I'm Ted Smith. I'm a doctor and I make $275,000 dollars a year.' 'I'm Susan Reed. I'm a teacher and I make $35,000.'"

As you might imagine, nobody liked Stanley's idea. "Why not?" he wanted to know. "You said you wanted to get biblical." "But income is private," was the answer given. "What I make is nobody else's business. That's between me and God."

Although I'm not advocating that congregations adopt Stanley's suggestion, it would certainly be an interesting and exciting exercise—an exercise that has a lot to do with this strange lesson from the Book of Acts. Peter's main contention with Ananias and Sapphira is *not* that they were wealthy, or really that they made a decision to withhold part of the sale of the land. "While it remained unsold, did it not remain your own? After it was sold," asks Peter, "were not the proceeds at your disposal?" (Acts 5:4).

The sin of Ananias and Sapphira is that they lie about their wealth and pretend that their offering was all they could afford. Peter uses this phrase twice. They "lie to the Holy Spirit" in verse 3 and "lie to God" in verse 4. Like this church couple who was ultimately (and literally) suffocated by their money, we too can delude ourselves into thinking that our offering is "all we can afford." An effective stewardship challenge honestly examines not what we give away, but what we keep; what we keep for our own family.

This old story about lying to God is indeed rather bizarre. But please don't misread it. This is not a story about God killing particular families for being greedy. It's a story about the consequences of greed and lying to God about our relative wealth. The story of Ananias and Sapphira is a cautionary tale warning Christian families that it's possible to be strangled by our wealth and possessions before we actually die.

≈

"Do not store up for yourselves treasures on earth, where moth and rust consume and where thieves break in and steal; but store up for yourselves treasures in heaven . . . For where your treasure is, there your heart will be also."

—Matthew 6:19–21

I offer here a couple of time-tested, basic maxims for life in the church: #1) If you're going to be a serious Christian, there's no getting around the fact that you're going to be a serious student of the Bible. Many people who join churches and remain members for years never come to terms with this first maxim. I suspect that most disagreements and misunderstandings in congregational life (regardless of denomination) emerge from basic lack of knowledge concerning the biblical story. Folks literally are not on the same page.

But even after you do become a serious student of scripture, you will no doubt bump headlong into maxim #2): Namely, the book we call Bible is a very strange, befuddling, head-scratching book. It is a "thick" book. And by that I do not mean that many Bibles weigh more than some newborn children. My Bible I use at home, for the record, weighs about five pounds. I weighed it not long ago. That's a lot of Bible, but that's not what I mean by "thick."

A hunk of scripture is thick when its interpretive density far outweighs our ability to understand what it means all at once and right away. Because we are used to "getting" something all at once or pretty quickly, it's easy to throw up our hands and turn to *TV Guide* after a long day of work. Because the Bible wallows in paradox, ambiguity, double entendre and this overall "thickness," it becomes tantalizingly easy to fill our lives with information that is infinitely more digestible and leaves us with (literally) less heartburn. In contrast, the Bible means to singe our hearts permanently.

Saint Paul's strange advice in 1 Corinthians 7:29–31 is a great example of what I would call a "thick" Bible text. Paul is writing to a congregation less than a hundred miles from Athens; a group of people struggling with how to be faithful to the crucified and risen Christ in a context of many competing theological and ethical options. In this regard, we're all Corinthians.

In this first letter, Paul has just addressed very practical issues that affect life in the congregation: sexuality, legal disputes, advice about marriage, family, and singlehood—earthy, everyday matters concerning their life together. Paul is eminently straightforward, understandable, and right to the point.

But then here comes the "thickness" of this text. Notice a phrase that appears five times in just three verses: "Brothers and sisters, the appointed time has grown short; from now on, let even those who have wives [or husbands, he would add] be *as though* they had none, and those who mourn *as though* they were not mourning, and those who rejoice *as though* they were not rejoicing, and those who buy *as though* they had no possessions, and those who deal with the world *as though* they had no dealings with it. For the present form of this world is passing away."

These are strange words, thick words, and may seem so otherworldly and bizarre to Christian families that Paul might very well be charged with escapism. Admittedly, Paul's words will not make much sense on first reading or fifth reading or in the time it takes to watch an episode of *Gilligan's Island*. His words are too strange, too demanding; in short, too thick. Often in reading the Bible, the first task is simply admitting one's personal befuddlement. How in the world can I live "as though" I'm not married if indeed I am?

Imagine the following conversation with my own wife. "Cindy, I realize I made those vows thirty years ago and everything, but from now on is it okay with you with if I pretend that I have no wife? If I live *as though* we really are not married? Just pretending now. Hypothetical. Do you have a problem with that?" How would this go over at your home even if you righteously quoted chapter and verse and the sanctions of St. Paul? Or how about this one: "Billy, I realize you loved your little hamster and all; and I certainly understand your tears on one emotional level, but according to Saint Paul you really need to let go of this and live *as though* this wasn't very sad at all. Get hold of yourself."

This is what I mean by a "thick" text. The challenge with Bible reading is not just to keep plowing through the pages (as if it's a race) and then we will all magically change through simple exposure to its inherent wisdom. "Well, I've read the whole Bible five times." No. One could profitably spend a few weeks with *just these three verses alone*.

Why does Paul talk this way? He says exactly why: "For the present form of this world is passing away." In other words, Paul seems to say, "Remember that you're not here all that long anyway. You're bound for another land. Place all earthly attachments in proper perspective." Paul is outlining for Christian households a sort of practice routine for another realm. He invites us to live "as though" because soon enough and for eternity, we will have none of the attachments that now command most of our attention.

Please understand. Paul is not saying that these earthly attachments are wrong. Nor is he saying that our commitments to family and our obligations to work should be shelved. Nor is he advocating some sort of fundamentalist removal from all earthly concerns until Jesus comes again. He is, however, pleading for a broader perspective and acknowledges how these earthly attachments can blind and distract us from living for the kingdom of God now.

Paul seems to suggest with panache and candor that all of our present earthly states will change soon enough. We are here for the time being. Every funeral we attend should be an opportunity for us to say, in truth, "Well, that's me one day soon enough." This is not morbid obsession. It is a candid reminder that our days here are numbered; Paul is inviting us to get in line with what God is doing in a much bigger picture than our normal daily concerns.

Usually we try and wedge a little religion into our busy days. Paul insists we've got it backwards. Our earthly attachments are temporary. *Live as though, live as though, live as though* . . . because soon enough this is how it truly will be.

I have to admit to you that I have a hard time living this way; answering the call of Jesus to place him first—above family, job, everything—as the first disciples seemed to do. They dropped everything and followed. I don't even come close.

My attachments are no doubt much like yours. I spend far too much money on my family in comparison to the family of God who is also my kin. I have lots more than I need. I hoard way too many possessions; my closets and pantry bulging in odd juxtaposition to the bulging stomachs of malnourished children, even though I'll be blessedly and rather ironically shed of this surplus in due time. I allow my emotions to define my days; whether a day is "good" or "bad" is directly related to how I "feel." I deal with the world in manipulative and shortsighted ways. God forgive me. Thank the Lord Lutherans have a confession and absolution each week.

Saint Paul provides a tonic for what ails us. Another perspective. *Live as though*, says the man. As though you no longer have any of these familiar things. It's coming—sooner than you think. What threatening (but ultimately loving) advice. Families might as well start practicing.

≈

My good friend Kent, a retired school teacher, lost his mother a couple of years ago. He went through what many have gone through with an aging parent: progressive dementia; the decision to place his mom in a nursing home; all of those very agonizing passages. After the funeral, a nephew moved into her old home in New Jersey. The family wasn't quite ready to sell the place with all of its memories and it wasn't a good time to sell anyway. There were few other assets besides the house and not many decisions to make. Several months passed.

One day Kent received a phone call from the nephew. "You're not going to believe this," he said. Investigating a plumbing problem under the sink that took him to the dark recesses of the kitchen cabinets, the nephew found hundreds of plastic bags stuffed far out of view. Each bag contained cash; some of it wet cash. When they counted all the money, the sum came to two hundred thousand dollars (you read that correctly), mostly in small bills. Kent's mom had been squirreling away money this way for at least three-quarters of a century. Her bank was hidden in her kitchen.

This was a story I heard over and again among old people when I served as a seminary intern in the mountains near Boone, North Carolina—life fortunes hidden behind the panel of a car door, or under a kitchen floorboard, or even in the ground. People didn't have to say why. They had lived through a Depression, and they were afraid.

What are you afraid of these days? Matthew tells a story (25:14–30) about a master returning from a long absence to settle accounts with three slaves. The first two are commended and the third is condemned to the outer darkness. What can we really conclude about this third guy given the evidence in the parable? Was he lazy? The master accuses him of laziness, but there is no evidence of such. He really doesn't seem to be such a bad guy, just careful. The master's blood really seems to boil upon hearing this line: "I was afraid, and I went and hid your talent in the ground" (25:25).

The master is so angry with this man that he throws him "into the outer darkness, where there will weeping and gnashing of teeth" (25:30). A fundamentalist preacher once delivered a sermon on this parable and chose to focus on the "gnashing of teeth" part of the story. In gruesome detail, the preacher vividly described the contours of such a dental hell—what it would be like and even sound like, such stereophonic gnashing from the throng. After worship that day, a toothless and guilt-ridden parishioner came through the line and asked what would happen to those who had no teeth to gnash. The pastor calmly responded, "Teeth will be provided."

"I was afraid," said the servant. Fear is a huge theme in the Bible. God is constantly sending angels to comfort hesitant followers with the phrase "Fear not." Fear is an utterly paralyzing emotion. Fear teaches us to always play it safe.

I recall a week-long bicycle trip on the Blue Ridge Parkway with friends, starting south of Asheville and back to where I lived at the time in Virginia. We discovered that a landslide had closed a portion of the Parkway near Mount Pisgah. I'd seen a picture of the landslide on the Internet only days before. It didn't look that bad to me. We arrived at the detour signs routing people down to Brevard, about forty miles out of our way. In a car, that's no sweat. On a fully-loaded bike, that's most of the day. It was Memorial Day and who would be working on a holiday? We chose to proceed down the Parkway and ignore the signs, more than once warning us to go back.

Upon finally reaching the landslide proper, we were greeted by heavy moving equipment and several glum men who were not so happy to see us. We picked our way through the rubble. "Watch the tunnels!" yelled the foreman from high up the slope above us. We soon discovered the source of his concern. Huge trucks were hauling tons of earth off the mountain. Because the road was officially closed, these truck drivers weren't really watching for bicyclists in the dark tunnels as they came up the mountain. Luckily, we all made it down safely. Here's what I learned from that incident: fear and bicycle speed are directly related. Later in the summer, I returned to that spot in a car and counted the number of tunnels between the landslide and the French Broad River where the road became officially open. I issued a quiz to my fellow bike riders. How many tunnels between the landslide and the river? Some riders said nine; others said five. There were actually only two. Fear multiplies fact every time. There were only two tunnels where we could have met our doom. I think that was worth the risk, don't you?

Why is fear such a commonly addressed theme in the Bible? God can work with sin by redeeming and forgiving it. But perhaps God cannot work with fear.

It has been commonly suggested that the opposite of faith is doubt. But in fact, I think doubt is a healthy companion to faith. Don't worry so much about your doubts. Doubt can be your theological friend. So what then is the opposite of faith? Here's my vote: the opposite of faith is fear. Why? *Because fear rules out possibility.* It closes us off to anything new. It closes the Christian family off to adventure. Nothing changes. We often live by what is controllable and knowable, acting only when reasonably sure of the outcome. Like that servant who buried his talent, we sometimes stick our heads in the ground, controlled by and afraid of the past, controlled by and afraid of embarrassment and failure. The master is galled by fear in this parable exponentially more than he is concerned about risk. Fear sends the master into orbit.

So how is fear affecting life in your household of faith these days? I think congregations should be constantly trying new things. One of the most paralyzing things we can possibly say in church life is also the most common: "That's the way we've always done it before." A lively church is a church that takes risks for the sake of the gospel. Think of the little boy with the loaves and fish. It was a huge crowd. And he didn't have a whole lot. It probably seemed like he was wasting what little he had. But he made the offering and Jesus did the rest.

It only follows that if a church, or families within the church, can act only when we're clear about the outcome, then why do we need God at all? You might remember it was Jesus the master who once said, "Those who want to save their lives will lose them and those who lose their lives for my sake will find them" (Matt 10:39). Maybe he didn't say anything about riding a bicycle into a dark tunnel, but I think you get my drift.

You know what? I really think that the returning master would have accepted *anything* but fear from that one servant. I think the master would have applauded him taking a chance and losing everything before digging a hole and playing it safe. Our Lord's life is decidedly not safe. It is anything but safe.

I counsel you to find another religion if you're uneasy about risk. Following Jesus is full of wild risks and decidedly uncautious acts. Religion without adventure is dead. Christ knew there were other resources, available from a divine source, that were far richer than those we hide in holes.

~

For several years I've saved a wonderful piece from *The New Yorker* titled "Confessions of a Pilgrim Shopaholic." Let me quote a bit:

> I am Rebecca, the wife of Mister Jonathan Harnsill. We arrived in the New World in 1626 and took up residence in a small cabin in the Plymouth Colony. Toward the end of our first January, I traveled to Boston to purchase a thimbleful of salt. And now, five years later, I have traveled to Boston for a second thimbleful. I am out of control. During our first winter, I sewed two simple black

> dresses, which I have alternated wearing in the years since. And yet this morning I find myself thinking about patching the frayed collar on one of the dresses. Have I no shame?[1]

Author Paul Rudnick was wise in choosing the pilgrim historical context to playfully expose a legalistic embrace of the biblical passages providing foundational theology for this chapter—Ananias, Sapphira, and Saint Paul's invitation to imagine a complete spiritual detachment from all possessions. Even though these passages involve life and death, we must play with them, even darkly laugh at them, lest their truths get lost in *deadly* legalism, fear, and a personal righteousness that seems holier-than-thou.

Rudnick's essay exposes the Pharisee in me who is grateful "that I am not like other people" (Luke 18:11). I'll always remember a speech aired on NPR given at the National Press Club by Millard Fuller, founder of Habitat of Humanity. Millard was recalling a speaking engagement at Pittsburgh Theological Seminary with about 200 pastors. He asked the assembled clergy: "Do you all think it might be possible to build a house so large that it's sinful in the eyes of God?" All 200 pastors raised their hands affirmatively. Millard continued. "Then at what precise square footage does the house become sinful?" No one responded for a few seconds. Finally, a pastor in the back of the room raised his hand. "When it's bigger than mine," he said.

Families contemplating faithful stewardship of wealth and possessions might profitably (pun intended) recall Fuller's story as they seek a way down the challenging yet liberating path of discipleship. Lutheran theologian Martin Marty somewhere says that living the Christian life is a lot like walking a tightrope between the dual pitfalls of cheap grace and works righteousness. It's easy to fall one way or another. The right place is on the tightrope—feeling the tension, the danger, and ultimately the exhilaration of living "as though."

1. Rudnick, "Confessions of a Pilgrim Shopaholic," 56.

6

Raising Children in the Faith

It's been ten years since we drove our oldest child, Hannah, to Staten Island, New York, to begin her freshman year at Wagner College, a Lutheran school perched high on the brow of a beautiful hill overlooking the New York City harbor. We helped her unpack, went to K-Mart to pick up a few forgotten items, ate lunch together, and said goodbye. Cindy and I wordlessly walked through the campus, holding hands, and back to our car that would take us on the long return journey to South Carolina.

I recall running into the Wagner school nurse on the walk back. She stopped us, I think, because she could tell we were both crying. We held it together back at the dorm, but must have looked a wreck there on the sidewalk. "Count your blessings," she said in that wonderfully thick Staten Island accent. "She'll be fine. Now my nephew—he was a freshman last fall at UConn? My brother drove him over to Storrs and they got to the dormitory but Jimmy wouldn't get out of the car—would not get out of that automobile. They had to circle the campus for at least an hour until my brother finally said, 'Now look, Jimmy, damn it. I've already paid a semester's tuition at this place and you're gettin' out of this car!'" She smiled beatifically at us as nurses sometimes do. "So count your blessings; count them." We never saw that nurse again in all our return visits to campus. But she told us exactly what we needed to hear that day. She told us the truth.

Depending on which scholar one consults, Samuel's exact age in his early encounter with Eli (1 Sam 3:1–21) is somewhat debatable. I've always enjoyed thinking that Samuel is a young impish lad of six or seven, puttering around the temple in his sandals and his little robe that his mom, Hannah, would drop off every year as he grew—such a dutiful, loving little boy who doted upon the near-blind priest Eli and pleased the old man more than his own sons.

I read a book[1] not long ago written by Randall Balmer, who teaches religion at Dartmouth College in Hanover, New Hampshire. Randall had a very dominant pastor father who wanted his son to grow up and preach the Word. There's a great picture in the book of Randall at age six, standing behind his birthday present that year: a miniature pulpit just his size, every hair in place with Vitalis. This is how I usually think about Samuel in our lesson—dutiful, obedient, cherubic, small; robed with his little slippers. A very, very good little boy.

So when little Samuel pads back and forth between the ark of God and his mentor's bedroom, he does so in childlike innocence. We see him trotting down the hall and tapping ever so softly on Eli's door. "Here I am, for you called me." Such a sweet lad. This is a Norman Rockwell moment.

But what if Samuel is a bit older than a little boy? Indeed, what if Samuel is a young adolescent or even an older teenager as some scholars think? It doesn't change Samuel's allegiance to Eli; that allegiance is unwavering regardless of age. But an older age might remove just a bit of Samuel's innocence and sweetness. And if so, I have to wonder if Samuel might have figured out whose voice is calling even before Eli makes the famous suggestion.

If Samuel is older, then I'm sure he's noticed already that all is not right in the temple of the Lord. I'm sure he's heard the stories about the sons of Eli (priests!) having sex with women on the temple grounds (1 Sam 2:22) and how the same clergy sons were economic scoundrels and took way more salary than they

1. Balmer, *Growing Pains*.

were due (2:12–14). Sex and money have always been our two big scandals, right? No surprise there.

So if Samuel was older, he was still an apprentice but he was not naive. He heard things. And he surely worried about the health of his mentor Eli, whose eyesight was so bad that he mistook Hannah for a drunk that day she came to pray (1:14) and whose weight was such a problem that it would contribute one day to Eli's own death (4:18). If Samuel is older, he knows there is hard truth to be spoken in this unhealthy family long before he hears the voice of God that night.

Here's a telling verse after Samuel's rather jarring visit from God, who reveals Eli's future demise: "Samuel lay there until morning" (3:15). This is fodder for the original Sominex commercial. "Then he opened the doors of the house of the Lord. Samuel was afraid to tell the vision to Eli." Insomnia, truth, and fear. Ever been there?

We may sense the need to change. We may know that things cannot continue as they are; an obviously dysfunctional situation. We may be keenly aware of whispers of illness in an individual or a family, even our own. And still we (like Samuel) may be slow to embrace the change, *even if the change is authored by God.*

Why is this? Well, very often, because we too are afraid. Afraid of the truth. Afraid, specifically, of the change the truth will bring. "Samuel was afraid to tell the vision to Eli."

Please notice that Samuel does not go bounding down the hall to finally share this truth. Eli almost has to drag the truth from him. Here's some more truth: it's easier not to speak the truth even when we know it must be spoken. Lots of forces assemble to help us hide the truth. Sometimes for years. Sometimes for life.

And so individuals, families, and even churches can perpetuate a conspiracy of silence because in some ways it's just easier to live with the dysfunction rather than deal with the change. At least the dysfunction is known and nameable. People, groups, organizations have lived with it for years, why not a little longer? Truth is a fearful thing, even when we know it needs to be stated. We shy away from truth at times because it's so disruptive.

"Samuel was afraid to tell the vision to Eli." It took a blind, old, overweight man whose time was up to draw from a young man what needed to be said. I'm glad Samuel had an older friend who helped him speak truth. It was almost like giving birth to something new, including the inevitable pain.

Part of the task of raising children in the faith is leading them to a community named church where the truth is spoken regularly, honestly, and lovingly. Truth and love are to be held together in tandem, according to Saint Paul (Eph 4:15). By only a couple verses, that expectation follows the remarkable possibility for a community to grow together "to maturity, to the measure of the full stature of Christ" (4:13). Paul seems to suggest that truth spoken in love is a key ingredient in arriving at such a stature. In my own experience as a parent and husband, it's very difficult to hold these two together. I can speak the truth occasionally, but hardly in love. Conversely, I can love without condition while fearing to speak the truth and live with its disruptive consequences. There's a bit of Samuel in all members of any family.

~

In our country, by their twelfth birthday, the average child in America has watched 30,000 television commercials. About forty-eight slick commercials a week (if my calculator is correct), which may be a low figure in many households. Multiply this figure accordingly for an adult who has reached forty or sixty and the number is exponentially higher.

We live in a world where we are saturated (I really don't think the word is too strong) with pitches to indulge ourselves, consume, and purchase products that will bring happiness and contentment. Even our toothpaste choice has seemingly eternal implications. You already know we live in such a world. This is not news.

Here's my central pastoral (and fatherly) concern given our present context: it's very doubtful that you'll see a commercial where some guy says anything even remotely approximating the following words. "If any want to become my followers, let them deny themselves and take up their cross and follow me" (Mark 8:34). (An aside: you might hear it on religious television, but the most successful preachers of the gospel on the tube usually will not touch this verse with a ten-foot pole. The gospel that really sells these days is one that promises financial success if you will only follow Jesus.)

Anyway, that verse (a core teaching of Christian discipleship) will never be the basis of a television commercial. And so a few questions are in order for all who love children with the specific love of Christ: Namely, where do we learn this teaching? And how do we muster the courage to actually live this way?

And an obvious answer is: "Well, you learn about that Jesus stuff in church." And that's surely a true statement. But here's what I want parents (and others) to struggle with mightily. When we compare 30,000 TV commercials by age twelve (and many more by age sixty) with the hour or two people manage to spend with Jesus (if we're lucky) on Sunday mornings, which message do you think is shaping American hearts and minds?

These words of Jesus are strange to our ears. "If any want to become my followers, let them deny themselves and take up their cross and follow me" (Mark 8:34). The words are honestly about as welcome as a loud burp at a debutante ball. In a recent winter Olympics, after reading of the endless self-absorption of one of our premier downhill skiers, it was so refreshing to hear another athlete say in an interview: "I'm not going to talk about myself today. I'm planning to give all my endorsement money from my medal, all of it, to the refugees struggling in Darfur. I hope it can help in the horrible situation in the Sudan."

Trust me: you will never hear this kind of thing on any commercial. And it's a plain rarity, period, in any media context. So again, *where do we hear* these words of Jesus? How often do we truly hear them compared to other words? And if they are (as I believe) a core description of the Christian life, how do we share these words lovingly (and truthfully, please recall) with members of our immediate family?

Early in the twenty-first century, we are in the midst of what theologians are calling a large "adaptive challenge" in the church. We must honestly confess that the Christian message in our congregations is often a proverbial drop in the bucket of commercial saturation in a setting that is frankly obsessed with the self. Whole generations are being formed and shaped by another compelling voice that encourages (nay, expects) us all to reflect endlessly upon our feelings, our self-esteem, our self-respect, our self-awareness, our self-image. There's even a magazine titled *Self* on the periodical market with many helpful tips to make the self-concerned self feel even better about ourselves. We love talk shows because the guests talk endlessly about, well, themselves.

You may recall that Peter (Mark 8:32) attempts to take Jesus aside and talk some common sense into this man who seems to be speaking like a lunatic. Jesus talks "openly" with the disciples and Peter throws a fatherly arm around Jesus' shoulder, takes him aside, and says, "Good grief man, lighten up a bit, would you? You can't be serious about all this." Peter was trying to domesticate Jesus. I do this all the time. In many ways, Peter is functioning as the wilderness Tempter in this scene. And Jesus honestly calls him just that. "Get behind me, Satan."

The text here then says that Jesus "turns" and looks at his disciples. Whenever Jesus slowly turns in the Bible, watch out. A theological bomb is about to drop. I imagine there was more than a moment's pause as Jesus turned and looked at his followers. The word used here to describe Jesus's terse response to Peter ("rebuke") is used elsewhere in the Gospel of Mark to quiet demons.

After dealing with Peter, Jesus calls the crowd together with the disciples. I suspect there was something less than a crowd after he spoke. "If any *want* to become my followers, let them deny themselves and take up their cross, and follow me." I stress that word "want" because it needs to be stressed. Jesus is describing what it means to be a disciple, but there can be *absolutely no coercion* in this invitation. Not a smidge of conversion coercion with Jesus. Jesus was indeed persuasive, but he was not coercive. If anybody ever tries to twist your arm into change, bully you into holiness, then whatever that is, it's not Christianity. It's important to remember this truth as children get older and take the important step of adopting and assimilating the faith into their own adolescent lives. "You'd better. You gotta. You should." These coercive words are not the words of Jesus. C. S. Lewis once wrote, "God cannot ravish. He can only woo."[2] This is sometimes a difficult truth for parents to absorb upon watching a young adult son or daughter walk away from the church. Jesus honestly describes what a Christian looks likes, act likes; but he can bully nobody into the kingdom. Parents should take our evangelical cues accordingly. "If any *want* . . ." At some point, desire to follow is assumed by Jesus. There will always be parental tension in this regard concerning how to pass on the faith to our children. Kenda Creasy Dean writes compellingly about Christian formation with adolescents, revealing the tension that emerges when issues of desire, encouragement, and coercion collide:

> American young people have learned a well-intentioned but ultimately banal version of Christianity that's been offered to them in American churches. Most youth seem to accept this bland view of faith as all there is—as something nice to have, like a bank account, something you have in case you need to draw from it in the future. What Christian adults have not told them is that this account of Christianity is bankrupt. We have not invested in their accounts: we "teach" young people baseball, but we "expose" them to faith. We provide coaching and opportunities for youth to develop and improve their pitches and their SAT scores, but we blithely assume that religious identity will happen by osmosis and emerge "when youth are ready" (a confidence we generally lack when it comes to, say, algebra).[3]

In a world where I'm constantly and eternally invited to be obsessed with "me," Jesus refreshingly reports that it's not about me after all. It's about the death of *me* in holy baptism (Rom 6:3–4)

2. Lewis, *The Screwtape Letters*, 23.
3. Dean, "Faith, Nice and Easy," 22.

and the rising of Jesus *in us*, the church. Our children must want that eventually themselves. At the same time, Dean reminds us, parents must clearly offer examples of faithful discipleship in an era where "following Jesus" can seem rather insipid and rote.

I recall a true story I ran across in a magazine several years ago. A man entered a jewelry store just before Easter looking for a cross for his wife. The young woman behind the counter slid back the glass partition housing the crosses. She laid them on the counter before the man. "Well," she said, "we have two kinds of crosses. The plain one and the one with the little man hanging on it."

That's the kind of story where you're not sure whether to laugh or cry.

Remember those 30,000 commercials. Our parental, truthful, but non-coercive challenge in raising children in the faith has never been so pressing.

~

To close this chapter on raising children in the faith I want to explore the old story of "the man born blind" found in John 9:1–41. This was a key conversion story (along with Nicodemus, the woman at the well, and the raising of Lazarus) used in the early church with catechumens preparing for baptism. Some of these stories found their way onto multiple catacomb walls. Many early liturgies (see the Hippolytus tradition, among others) reveal a protracted conversion process that lasted up to three years. Authentic conversion to the ways of Christ takes time and effort. Jesus cannot be wedged between soccer and piano lessons with any lasting effect. I recently noticed seven distinct scenes in this long story.[4]

Scene One—Yeah, I hear you. If somebody came at me with a gooey, phlegmy glob of muddy paste I'm not sure I could sit still, even if I was blind. Jesus hocks and spits and makes mud, almost like a little child playing around in the backyard. My mother tells me I used to eat mud in Chattanooga as a little boy; she'd catch

4. It might be helpful to have an open Bible here.

me time and again, scooping it from the high bank on the other side of the back alley. Maybe I was searching for some missing and needed mineral in my youthful diet; some element from the periodic table.

There's something about Jesus bending there in the dirt that reminds me of that tender scene in Genesis where God stoops down in the primordial dust, scoops up a handful of earth and breathes life into the first human. Something new is happening here. *Creation* is occurring. "Go wash in the pool," says Jesus. The blind man with the less-than-hygienic mud in his eyes obeys. He washes and he sees. "I once was blind but now I see," wrote the author of the famous hymn, a man who once trafficked in slaves. Washing and seeing. This is the language of baptism, although the word is never used in this long forty-one verse story.

But that's John's metaphorical way in this old Gospel. Anytime you come across a reference to water or food in John, think sacraments. John is arguably the most sacramental of all the Gospels, but not overtly. He drops a lot of hints in this regard. Something new is happening here. A new creation with dust and spit and water—elemental building blocks of life.

Scene Two—It doesn't take long for the news to get around town and, of course, nobody believes it. "Isn't this the guy who used to shake his tin cup and beg for coins down on the corner?" "You know, I can understand your confusion because he does really resemble that guy—a lot in fact; the hair is almost exactly and impeccably the same—but it's a totally different guy. You need to have your eyes examined." "Look people," said the once-blind man, "we've been neighbors all our lives, right? You see me every day. I couldn't see you, of course, until now—and you're coming more into focus all the time. But come on. It's me, it's really me. How? Well, this guy (you're not going to believe this) put mud on my eyes and I went and washed. Where is he? Well, come to think of it, I don't really know."

Those who now see with the eyes of Jesus have a similar problem to this man who used to shake a tin cup and beg down on the corner. When questioned about our new sight in Christ by others—Well, where is he? Where'd he go? When's he gonna show up again?—we recognize in many ways that we're in the same boat. We're between the coming of Jesus and his coming again. Most of the action in this old story occurs without the presence of Jesus. He heals the blind man and exits stage left until the very ending of the story. I think this will undoubtedly be our experience in this in-between time; perhaps a challenge in passing on the faith to our children who live in such a visual world.

We have his word, of course. We have the promise of his presence in the sacraments. But an exact and precise explanation of our life in Christ and a precise and confident pinpointing of the location of Jesus at all times is going to elude us here in the meantime in-between. And it will make the task of sharing the faith all the more challenging in our skeptical world. "Where is he then with Japan's tsunami, Newtown, fill-in-the-blank?" "Well, I'm not really sure," said the once-blind man. There are answers to these old questions even in new settings. But they will always be partial and in-between answers.

Scene Three—Please don't dump on the Pharisees in this next scene. They are simply defending tradition. You could probably just insert here the word "Lutherans" or "Lutheran pastors" or even the name "Frank Honeycutt" for the word "Pharisees." They/I/we call the man downtown to synod headquarters for a friendly interrogation. We don't buy his story for a minute. He may as well have seen the Virgin Mary singing "Ave Maria" at the top of her lungs halfway up an oak tree over in Conyers, Georgia. We are dubious because that is our nature and so we ask the poor guy to repeat his story (yet *again* with the mud and the water and the washing) but the hint of my smirk is discernible even as I try to listen politely. And this is our challenge, right?

Sometimes it's a challenge for people like us—Christians with a wonderful and rich tradition—to know what an authentically real and new movement of the Holy Spirit might actually look like in a year such as 2013. Why? Because we (I) want to closely guard and honor the tradition. The Pharisees are agitated and worked up here. But don't dump on them too hard. They serve as a mirror for us who distrust anything new in religious life.

Scene Four—This scene is perhaps the most tragic and sad of all in this old story of tragedy and sadness. No one thus far has rejoiced with this once-blind man. No alleluia, no backslap, no prayer of thanksgiving from a neighbor or old friend or religious leader. Not even a word of gladness from his mother or father! And if the man was "born blind" then that means his parents had lived with this challenge since they held their son in their arms as an infant. "We have no idea how he sees," they answer when questioned. "Go ask him. He's over twenty-one now, you know."

I think the parents here are certainly afraid of the synagogue police. But there's more. We sometimes underestimate the change and the division that Jesus can bring to family life. Baptism shifts allegiance. I am no longer (primarily) child of Bob and Ruth Honeycutt. In baptism, I am child of *God*. This primary allegiance to God does not mean that I will abandon family commitments, but it does put those commitments in perspective within the context of God's family. I sometimes think we should perform baptisms in churches with an accompanying warning label. The child or adult is signing on with a brand new family.

Scene Five—Back downtown, the once-blind man undergoes interrogation number two. I see a dark room illumined with a single light; inquisitors in the shadows: "What did he do to you? How did he open your eyes? Where does he come from?" All these rapid-fire questions that begin to test the patience of our hero. He's becoming a little uppity. Good for him. "Look, I've told you people this story about seven times. Why in the world would you want to hear it again? Are you interested in signing on as one of his disciples?" And with this last question, something snaps in those who thought they were in control. "Look, you little whippersnapper, who do you think you're talking to here? We know more about God than you do. We make the rules around here." And they drove him out.

Scene Six—The isolation is now complete. And still no hallelujah, no congratulations, no party, and not even a greeting card to celebrate the good fortune of this man blind from birth. And top off that reality with this: neighbors, friends, parents, and even his religious guides have all let him down; no one comes to his defense.

It is at the height of this isolation that Jesus re-enters the story, as if to underscore what the man has lost, finally helping him celebrate the movement he is entering. "Lord, I believe." And his sight becomes fully clear.

In many years of reflection on this narrative, this is the first time I've noticed that the story has six very distinct scenes and then ends. I got to thinking about that number, the imperfect number six in the Bible. I smile now while writing these words because I really wouldn't put it past the author of the Gospel of John to be sending a little message from his vantage point to ours, even with all the centuries in between.

We are living out **Scene Seven**. The church in every age. And even though the history and context might change, the issues are the same: spiritual blindness, baptismal washing, resistance to change, the absence and presence of Jesus, and the new family that is the church.

We are living the seventh scene. "Surely we are not blind, are we?"

It's not a bad question to ponder as parents and caregivers of the children in our care.

7

Spiritual Maturity and Conversion at the Home Address

NOT LONG AGO I participated in a rather remarkable long-distance phone call. One of our church members, Mike, was dying in a Boston hospital of a rare form of lung cancer. He gathered his family around his bedside for a two-hour conversation about what's important in this life, things to keep central during hectic and distracting days. Mike requested the Lutheran version of "last rites" to be scheduled with me for the next day, over the phone, many states separating us geographically.

Several months prior, I'd met Mike at his home and we set out on a walk together. In the middle of the walk, Mike stopped for a short rest. He looked at me and said, "It's such a gift, isn't it?" And at first I didn't quite catch on, so he said, "This ability to breathe. Have you ever thought about what all has to occur just to take your next breath? What all God had to devise?" And I had to confess to Mike that day that indeed I had not thought about that lately. And really not in a long time. "Cancer," he said, "has taught me to look at this one day. Just this day, this moment, this next breath." And his smile was as wide as the sky.

We prayed the Commendation of the Dying, connecting Boston and South Carolina, over the phone. A daughter traced Mike's brow with a cross, the same cross that marked him long ago at baptism. At the conclusion of the rite, I'm on the phone with

Jon, Mike's son, ready to hang up on my end here in Walhalla. But Jon says, "Pastor Frank, can you wait a minute? Dad wants to talk to you." And for a moment there, with some of the last breaths he would take in this life, Mike was the minister—thanking me, encouraging me, telling me that God would be with me as a pastor. He died a couple hours after we hung up. That conversation left me shaking my head in wonder and thanksgiving. And a question slowly emerged: How do we foster a household climate where such mature actions of grateful love pervade all the stages of this life, even death itself?

≈

With some regular frequency, in a variety of his letters to fledgling churches, Saint Paul asks people to copy his own lifestyle; to duplicate in their own lives how he has chosen to live. At least six times he says things like, "Be imitators of me." "Be imitators of me, as I am of Christ." "You yourselves know how you ought to imitate us."[1]

Writing from jail, Paul urges the church in Philippi to "join in imitating me and observe those who live according to the example you have in us" (Phil 3:17). In other words, Paul is inviting people to watch him closely, follow him around, and learn from him how to become a disciple of Jesus. "Imitate me," he says. "Copy the way I do it." He offers his own life as a textbook in the Christian way.

Even though it's been said that "imitation is the most sincere form of flattery," it's hard for modern Christians to offer their lives to others in this way. Perhaps you remember the old Michael Jordan Gatorade commercial where kids were encouraged to "Be Like Mike." But can you imagine some ad campaign in my home congregation that urges people to "Be Like Frank"? I wouldn't like that. Neither would you, I suspect, in your own church. But *why* wouldn't we like it? *Why* wouldn't we want our lives to be lifted up as worthy of imitation? Well, here are three reasons that come to mind.

1. See, for example—1 Cor 4:16, 11:1; 1 Thess 1:6; 2 Thess 3:7, 9.

First, I suppose I wouldn't want anyone looking too closely at my obvious flaws on a regular basis. I spend a lot of time hiding and justifying these flaws. It would raise a fair amount of stress in my week if I thought someone was peering too closely into my life, especially my private life, and discovering what a failure I really am at various aspects of discipleship. If someone were to follow me around, for example, shadow me wherever I go, hoping to learn about Jesus by mimicking me, it might be a bit embarrassing at the end of a few months to realize that they had not progressed very far.

Second, here in America we often look down on anything that remotely smacks of imitation. We don't like imitation leather or imitation jewelry or imitation orange juice. We appreciate "the real thing." We value that which is unique—especially one-of-a-kind occurrences and people. It's professional suicide in the recording or entertainment industry (or even in politics) if you happen to sound like somebody else. Strive to be fresh and new, and you'll go far in life.

Ponder these sentences that have been elevated to something approaching a national creed: "No two of us are exactly alike. We have unique spirits, similar to snowflakes that fall—no two bearing the same image. I'm special. There's no one else exactly like me." Now there may be some truth in this creed, but in such a context, imitation is not only discouraged, it's usually perceived as just plain wrong.

Third (and this is similar to number two), there is something inside of me, perhaps pride, that doesn't want to ask for help from somebody else; something inside of me that wants to figure life out all by myself. To offer an overused example: it's probably why most men won't ask for directions. Men and women are born with a fierce independence that says at an early age, "Let *me* do it, Daddy/Mommy. *By myself*." And, of course, such independence is undeniably good—it will take a person far. I simply note this third point because there is probably at least a mild built-in resistance in our lives to learn from others. And if that is true, then we may resist imitation because we'd rather figure things out on our own. Sing along: *I GOTTA BE ME! I GOTTA BE ME!* (Sorry about that.)

There are probably other reasons why we'd feel uncomfortable running a church ad campaign putting forth our own lives as Christian models of virtue, worthy of imitation. I didn't even mention the risk of arrogance. Maybe Saint Paul could get away with saying, "Imitate me," but who really has the chutzpah to say such a thing today?

In America today, we are so incredibly respectful of individual choice and individual freedom that it makes us hesitant to offer up our own lives as an example for others. I sometimes meet parents who are so afraid of passing on values to their children because they want their children to make up their own minds. As if they were really capable of doing this at age five without our guidance.

Here's just one example I hear a lot: "I don't want to shove religion down little Johnny's throat. I want him to . . . choose." But choose between what? From religion to sex to how we spend our money, we often deny the very real and vital role we have in helping our young make important decisions. "I want her to choose for herself. I want him to decide."

There is perhaps no other period in the history of the Christian church where young people, and others new to the faith, need opportunities to "apprentice" under a seasoned Christian—to watch mature disciples, follow them around, peer closely into their lives *and imitate them*. When seekers come to your church looking for Jesus, you might hand them the Bible; you might hand them appropriate books and resources and classes. But if you aren't able to hand them living, breathing, mature disciples worthy of emulation, then you know what? We're in a heap of trouble. And to go a step further: even though we might not like it, people new to the church are looking at our lives anyway, trying to get some sense of the presence of Jesus.

I've always appreciated this quote from Jim Wallis of the Sojourners community in Washington, D.C. He says, "Our scriptures, confessions, and creeds are all very public, out in the open.

Anyone can easily learn what it's supposed to mean to be a Christian. Our Bible is open to public examination; so is the church's life. That is our problem. People can read what our scriptures say, and they can see how Christians live. The gulf between the two has created an enormous credibility gap."[2] Perhaps this is our greatest fear in the realm of imitation: the fear of others discovering this credibility gap in our own lives.

From a distance, from jail, and in tears, Saint Paul wrote some bold advice for a young church. This church was surrounded by a culture whose "god is the belly" (Phil 3:19). And even though we don't know exactly what he meant by that, I think it's fairly easy to guess. Paul's advice for such a church? "Join in imitating me, and observe those who live according to the example you have in us." Remember that Paul didn't have a New Testament to hand these people; he could only hand them his life—even a flawed and sinful life.

We live today in a culture whose god is also "the belly"—our appetites are legion. How do we reclaim our young people, who (in many cases) are raising each other much of the time? If you ask me, Paul's advice still stands. We offer our very lives for examination and even imitation. We dare to hold each other accountable. Like it or not, we are being watched anyway by many pairs of eyes.

Ultimately, if our lives cannot lead people to Jesus, if I am hesitant to offer my own life as evidence of the resurrection, then a bushel of sermons, a year's worth of Sunday school classes, and any number of creative evangelism pitches will eventually fall on deaf ears. With Saint Paul, we freely offer our very lives as evidence of the living Christ.

~

The following reflection was first shared as a letter to Haileigh, Alex, and Rachel, three ninth-graders in our church on the day of their

2. Wallis, *The Call to Conversion*, 18–19.

confirmation as they affirmed their common baptism before the congregation.

When I was in the sixth grade, I was a very good student—one of the best at Elbert Long Elementary School in Chattanooga. I made all A's, all the time. Nothing less. Ever. My teachers praised me and told my mother, who taught fourth grade just down the hall, what a good student I was.

Well, one morning in October, I went to class and there was a test. And I was totally unprepared, which wasn't like me. I can't remember if I just forgot about the test or whether it was a pop quiz, but I do remember this great feeling of panic because I wasn't ready, caught completely off guard. What was I going to do? I had this academic reputation to protect and everything.

There was this tall, lanky kid named John who sat in front of me. I was sitting there that morning sweating buckets, looking at the questions as if they were written in Chinese, and John appeared to be sailing through the quiz with no problems. I always thought John was sort of a nerd and I, of course, was in the popular group. We didn't have a whole lot to do with each other, and I wouldn't have even been sitting near the guy if the teacher hadn't assigned the seats. But on that particular morning, John looked to me like the Savior of the world. Or, at the very least, like my own personal Savior.

So for the first and last time in my life, I looked on a paper that wasn't mine and said, "Hey, John, what'd you get for number 6?" And he told me, gave some sign that would never be noticed. "And while you're at it, how about number 4? 9? 12?" And it was so easy, like taking candy from a baby. The teacher was never the wiser and the next day, just as before, my paper came back with the familiar "A" at the top of the page and an affirming note about my own good work. My reputation was intact and John and I, new cohorts, laughed at recess about how we'd put one over on the teacher.

No one ever discovered our secret as the days passed towards Thanksgiving and then Christmas. But I knew. And what I had done slowly grew bigger and darker than the embarrassment of a tarnished academic reputation. I couldn't eat or sleep because of what I'd done. I felt so guilty with this great weight of shame. In my sixth-grade imagination this ten minutes of cheating came to have equal moral repulsion as the behavior of a bank robber.

For weeks I carried around this guilt until I just couldn't take it anymore and one Saturday morning I slowly walked into my mother's bedroom as if it were a gas chamber and just poured out the whole sordid tale all at once. I would rather face her wrath than my own guilt. Guilt can be a horribly heavy thing, no matter your age. You can feel like the whole world is looking at you, like that Chicago Cubs fan who touched the foul ball several years ago by mistake and ruined things for a whole city. Shame can be horribly heavy. I was in such anguish, just on the verge of tears.

The story poured out fast like dammed water released through a spillway. To this day I can remember being sort of surprised at how much better I felt for having told someone about my secret. And I remember my mother's hug; remember her voice. "It's okay, it's okay," she said. "I think you've suffered enough with this. You'll know what to do next time."

You know that part of the service we do every week at the very beginning? The confession? That has become a very powerful few moments for me, maybe my favorite part of the service. Because in the confession, and again at the Lord's Table, I'm reminded that there is a God who can read my heart like a book and knows all about all the guilt hidden there. A God who says, "It's okay, it's okay. I think you've suffered enough with this. You'll know what to do next time." I'm reminded in confession that I don't have to pretend to be perfect.

And, you know, we live in a world where there's a lot of pressure to try and *be perfect*. All three of you have probably experienced something of that by now. There seems to be a pecking order in school (and sometimes in life) where the perfect-looking people with the perfect clothes and perfect grades and the girls who look like Victoria's Secret models and the guys who make all the sports teams seem to get all the attention and seem so perfectly happy all the time. The truth of the matter is that all people, even those who strive the most for perfection and seem so perfectly happy, very often drag secrets around that they hide from everybody but God—who can see into hearts and knows that sometimes those who seem the happiest are often the saddest people of all.

One of the clearest truths in the Bible, a truth that is handed down to us anytime we celebrate a baptism, is that God sees differently than we do. If you three guys remember only one thing from your confirmation day, this is what I hope you'll remember: God doesn't love us according to all these external things like clothing and wealth and good looks and grades and these things on the outside that so many people seem to think are so important. God's eyes see where no one else can—God sees into our hearts and knows what is going on with us no matter how we try to hide it.

Now this might seem like bad news to you; that God can see this way, maybe ready to pounce on our mistakes or something. But actually, it's wonderful news. The Bible reading from Jeremiah assigned for today reminds us that for a long time God tried to impose God's will on us from the outside in. But no more. "I will put my law within them," says God, "and I will write it on their hearts" (Jer 31:33). God knows all the secret places of your heart.

I hope the three of you will remain active in the church as the years go by. Not just because you will make promises today to do so. And not just because you guys have so many gifts and talents that the church can use to further the mission of Christ. But mainly because each of you, and all of us here as a matter of fact, are a lot like that sixth-grade boy who got away with a lie but couldn't live with it.

Even when we are successful at hiding our mistakes, God sees deeply into our hearts—not to increase our guilt or somehow catch us, but to forgive us, to accept even our imperfections. God is like a loving mother who says, "It's okay, it's okay. You've suffered enough with this. You'll know what to do next time."

Many blessings to all three of you on your special day. You are about to stand where so many others have stood before. Smack dab between font and altar, the great mercy seat of God, the very place where Christ writes his love upon our hearts.

God's Peace to each of you,
Pastor Frank

≈

I recall as a child how many of the Christians in my life seemed to have life itself so thoroughly figured out. They made mistakes, of course, but mostly I was only able to guess at the details. I came to associate Christianity with the attainment of perfection. Christian maturity is an important thing to strive for and imitate. But so many families disintegrate because the mistakes of a family (held up to the perception of unrelenting high expectations by a judgmental Jesus) are never dealt with in an open and healthy way. I close this chapter on maturity in the Christian household with a very old story. Sometimes it's those who are well down the path of "obedience" and maturity who have the most to learn in family life.

≈

When I was a much younger father I was convinced that I should have gone to law school. *He got a little more ice cream than I did. No fair! Why does she always get to stay up a half-hour later than I do? That's favoritism, that's not fair! She got to sit in the front seat last time. It's not fair that I always have to sit in the back. I'm always having to clean up my room and his looks like a pig sty—no fair!*

An effective parent often needs the wisdom of a judge and the memory of an elephant. Wisdom to hand down rulings at the drop of a hat in a variety of public and private settings, and a memory to recall past court cases in order to project at least the illusion of fairness to all parties involved. The domestic *quid pro quo.*

This principle of fairness has a very large hold on us, and if you think we eventually outgrow the moral outrage of being denied something clearly deserved or expected, then think again. I've seen strangers argue over a parking space. I once observed family members get into a major tiff over mom's will not thirty minutes after her funeral service. I've seen divorces finally settled with both parties about to kill the other—all over issues of fairness.

And you might say, "Oh, I would never do that." Really? Have you ever had the experience of sitting patiently in traffic on the Interstate, waiting your turn in line to navigate around the accident? And here comes some road hog in the rearview who intends to blow right past everyone else who's been waiting. I don't know about you, but I often try to cut him off. It's not fair.

So I have a hunch. Maybe you did a crazy thing or two in your past, sowed your share of wild oats perhaps, grateful to be taken back and forgiven. But I'm guessing that you probably identify on most days with the older brother in the old story of two sons and a loving father (Luke 15:11–32). Why is the older brother so mad? Well, you know why.

As the sun sets on this story, what has the older brother been doing all day? All month? Probably all of his adult life? Well, he's been working his butt off, to put it bluntly. He is exhausted, his boots smell of cow poop, and he could certainly use a shower. He's been doing his own work and probably the work of his deadbeat brother for weeks now. You want to talk about fairness? Well, the older brother, understandably so, has been keeping a mental ledger for some time. Any of us would. But here's what I think really sends the old boy over the edge.

On his way in from work that night, he hears about the return of the rapscallion. Somebody even breaks the news about the incredibly excessive trinity of welcome for his jerk brother—robe, ring, and fatted calf. But this is what really makes the older brother snap: he hears "music and dancing," and not just a fiddle and banjo player. The Greek word here for "music" is *symphonia*. The older brother hears a virtual orchestra of instruments. A symphony. This is not just chips and dip with a six-pack. This is quite an elegant party.

So search yourself deep down. Had you been there; had you been working your rear end off for months; had your father thrown an extravagant party for someone who clearly did not deserve one—would you have gone in? And if not, why not? Well, I think we all know why. All together now: *it wasn't fair*.

Martin Luther was fond of saying that this old story was the "granddaddy" of all parables. The word "parable" comes from two Greek words—*para* (meaning "alongside") and *bolle* (meaning "to throw"). A "parable" is literally something that is *thrown alongside* something else, with the intention of causing friction and sparks. The friction here is obvious. The delightful thing about a parable is that Jesus hardly ever wraps up his stories with a neat bow of explanation; they're almost always rather open-ended.

For example, we never know if the man in the ditch ever expresses gratitude for the excessive care of a Good Samaritan. We never learn if those who worked a full day in the vineyard (and got paid exactly the same wage as those who worked only an hour) ever got over their anger. And we never learn if this older brother ever does much more than cross his arms in righteous fury and refuse to go into the party. A cloud of hurt feelings follows him around, maybe forever. A parable works because if we really hear it, the story will highlight a friction point in our own lives. And I suspect you might be thinking of one right now as you read these words. Jesus was a shrewd storyteller. He does not provide an obvious and unmistakable ending. We are living out the ending each time we hear the story.

Back to the older brother, listening to the *symphonia* in the growing shadows of the day with his arms crossed in righteous refusal. He's mad. Oh, he is ticked. See him there? But as evening comes on, let me ask another question. Who raises the real ire of this older brother? He may be disgusted with the behavior of a sibling, but who really makes him spitting mad here as the curtain closes? Well, the father is the recipient of his son's hot words and pointed barbs. The father receives a tongue-lashing for his misguided generosity. The father catches an earful and is charged with blind merit and favoritism. The elder son is mostly ticked off at his dad.

At the end of the Civil War, Abraham Lincoln was asked: "How are you going to treat these rebels?" Lincoln replied, "I'm going to treat them as if they never went away." God's radical welcome of sinners may be good news for some, but more likely, it's bad news for many. God is great and God is good. But let me level with you: *God is not fair*. Christ will "come again to judge the living and the dead." But if the judgment even approximates the behavior of the dad in this old story, it might just make you spit nails. C. S. Lewis once said, "God will accept anyone in heaven who can stand it."

For God loves sinners; is crazy about sinners. Among the lavish gifts heaped upon the wayward son is a ring. The word "ring" appears only here (Luke 15:22) and one other time in the entire New Testament. A ring, of course, is a sign of fidelity and unconditional love. The main message here may be that God the Father is wedded to a sinful world, through thick and thin, never giving up on anyone.

Are there no limits to his forgiveness? Does God welcome just anybody to the banquet table of welcome and grace? *But that's not fair*. And so the parable continues just as Jesus intended, in your life and mine, delightfully open-ended.

Sometimes I'm the prodigal. And sometimes I'm the older brother with arms crossed in self-righteousness—would that both sides of me come to embrace the God who, thankfully, is never fair.

~

Both gift and occasional liability, the human family is potentially the central locus for permanent and lasting damage in any of our lives. Hardly a day goes by in my pastoral work where I don't hear of fallout between siblings or a strained relationship between parent and child that has lasted for months, even years. "We don't speak to each other anymore." Reconciliation is often agonizing work that takes decades of time to fully bloom.

At the same time, the human family has vast potential as a primary context for Christian maturity and growth. Family is where we learn to imitate the eccentricities of an offbeat uncle who loves Jesus. Family is where we experience the open wounds caused by harsh words and thoughtless actions, but also where we discover the great power of confession and forgiveness. Family is where we make colossal mistakes, but also where we learn to live and love through an unexpected grace that comes from completely outside ourselves, authored by a Lord who grew up in a household that resembled ours in many key ways. Imitation, confession, and return—these are the marks of Christian maturity. The family is a kind of "discipleship lab" where we learn how to make headway in all three.

8

Why Jesus Has More in Mind than Mother's Day

"When Jesus saw his mother and the disciple whom he loved standing beside her, he said to his mother, 'Woman, here is your son.' Then he said to the disciple, 'Here is your mother.' And from that hour the disciple took her into his own home."

—John 19:26–27

During his long and productive writing career, John Cheever (1912–82) occasionally taught writing workshops in New York state prison settings. Here's how one inmate describes the experience:

> "Cheever, you understan', he was a brilliant writer. When he wrote something, he always had two things going on at a time. He told us, when you writin', you got this surface thing, you understan', goin' on up *here*"—he moved his left hand in a circle with his fingers spread apart, as if rubbing a flat surface—"an' then once you got that goin' on, now you got to come *under* it"—he brought his right hand under his left, as if throwing an uppercut—"come *under* this thing here that's goin' on up here, you understan'. That's how John Cheever said you write."[1]

1. Frazier, "Hungry Minds," 58.

Likewise, this is pretty much how Jesus taught and preached as he wandered the hills of Galilee and invited others to follow. His teachings about the kingdom of God, specifically how we live in relation to one another as particular members of a family, are filled with double entendre, multiple meanings, and delightfully open endings. The word "family" in the wide-ranging lexicon of Jesus always attempts to recast blood kin relationships through the gospel prism of baptism. Jesus's rather strange words spoken to his mother from a cross would not have been lost on her as she listened to her son's take on family life over the years. "Here's your new mother; here's your new son." Makes perfect sense through a baptismal lens. With the word "family," Jesus is always coming "under this thing that's goin' on up here." It makes for an interesting Mother's Day no matter how you try and parse Jesus's words.

≈

In the middle of the state of Pennsylvania there is a place called Pine Grove Furnace State Park. The Appalachian Trail runs through it and most hikers consider the park the traditional halfway point—1,000 miles down and 1,000 to go. To celebrate this little milestone a club was established many years ago called "The Half Gallon Club" and the idea is to sit down with a half-gallon of your favorite flavor of ice cream and consume the whole thing in one sitting.

I know it sounds nauseating but you have to recall that balancing the consumption of so many calories is the burning of so many in any given hiker day. If a hiker completes the task successfully your name goes up on the wall in the little state park general store. You pay for your half-gallon, sit down at a picnic table, dig in with a sturdy spoon, and hope for the best.

Almost as enjoyable as eating the ice cream is reading the logbook of those who sign in and describe their frozen culinary experience. I remember reading a variety of amusing ordeals from the summer of 1984, the year I hiked through, but my hands-down favorite in the logbook was very brief, consisting of the date and just two words: "Avoid nuts."

I suppose we've been hearing that little adage of wisdom all our lives. Avoid strange and suspicious people. Avoid unusual ideas. Avoid anything that upsets the status quo. Avoid nuts.

But it's precisely people who have seemed a little nutty at the time who shaped human history. And our list would probably differ as to who might be included in that lineup, but what they all have in common is a certain outrageous perspective and behavior that was just, well, out-of-step and strange in their day, and maybe still is.

One thing the church in any century needs to come to terms with is that Jesus is the King of Nuts. He said impossibly weird things and invited his followers to live in very strange ways. And if you've never felt any of this strangeness or experienced any of this weirdness, I'd have to conclude that you and I are just reading different Bibles. Jesus will always be a bit of a nut when we drop him into a wine and cheese glass-tinkling gathering, or a high school hallway between classes, or the summer family reunion at the beach. We can deal with his strangeness in worship perhaps; it's over and we're outside soon enough. But try living Jesus's way in all respects. And here's a promise: people will think you're nuts. His teachings just do not fly in so many contexts. But his nutty-sounding words concerning our most treasured relationships can bring health and direction to families in a new century. His words can save us from ourselves.

~

It's a Tuesday afternoon in late July and I'm standing in the middle of the Chattooga River of *Deliverance* fame, the watery border between South Carolina and Georgia. I could easily throw a small stone into the so-called Peach State. Elizabeth, our youth director, wedges her hindquarters into a rock crevice alongside a small but very swift rapid in the river. Bryce, a tenth-grader in our group, jumps into a deep eddy, grabs Elizabeth's extended foot with his right arm and reaches out with his left to assist a dozen youth and adult leaders as they shoot gleefully through the narrow channel of water.

July twenty-eighth (Bach's death date) is my baptismal anniversary and as I step back from the action and take in the symphony of slippery bodies, primal squeals, and all that rushing water, I'm reminded of how the church brings new Christians to birth—connected and anchored; collectively. My New Testament professor in seminary, Dr. Sigel, was fond of saying that Southerners understand the Eucharist better than most because we embrace unambiguous expressions of the plural pronoun: "The Body of Christ given for y'all." Sometimes it's tough for teenagers to articulate their baptismal identity in this ancient body, especially given our immersion in a culture offering deceptive pitches suggesting who we are or might be. In his excellent book, *Faith Forming Faith*, Paul Hoffman writes that for many Christians "the *act* of baptism [is] equated with salvation, but not necessarily with ongoing life in Christ through the ministry of the Church . . . only gift, no responsibility."[2] This may certainly be true with a new generation of youth who often were brought forward to a font by well-meaning relatives only for some dimly-understood purpose of spiritual "protection."

Shadows fall in the gorge earlier than back in town. The Chattooga is a National Wild and Scenic River. Cell phones don't work here, far from any human structure or convenience. We collect and purify water, set up tents, fire up the small stoves, go over safe bathroom etiquette, play charades, and hungrily down Lipton chicken and rice. A torrential electrical storm will sweep through camp later in the night, absolutely soaking through one of the girls' tents, but for now we hunker down by the fire, listen to the river play tag with the deep forest sounds, and dive into the Gospel of Luke.

Fifteen of us are here for our congregation's annual three-day youth backpacking trip along the Foothills Trail to reflect upon our baptismal calling; also raising money and awareness for the ELCA

2. Hoffman, *Faith Forming Faith*, 36.

World Hunger Appeal. This is the same trail where I almost lost Boyce a couple years earlier. Even with that old memory, it's worth it to get teenagers away from their iPods and help them completely unplug. It's hard to get their attention with all the gadgets, even on Sundays, and nice to be in a context where the Word can truly sink in like summer rain. More and more Christian educators are questioning the real impact of Sunday School on adolescent faith development and touting outdoor settings as possibilities with at least as much potential for real and lasting discipleship.

Kenda Creasy Dean, in her book *Almost Christian*, compellingly writes about why youth are leaving the church; not because of disinterest or hostility but due to what they perceive as "benign whatever-ism" in the faith of the church's adults: "If we fail to bear God's life-altering, world-changing, fear-shattering good news (which, after all, is the reason the church exists in the first place)—if desire for God and devotion to our fellow human beings is replaced by a loveless shell of religiosity—then young people unable to find consequential Christianity in the church absolutely *should* default to something safer. In fact, that is exactly what they are doing."[3]

We take safety precautions on this trip, of course, but also want to push the comfortable boundaries of our daily lives a bit. It's unfortunate that many of us have grown up with the image of "Sallman's Christ" as the dominant artistic rendering of the Savior, a man who looks like he just stepped out of the shower with a Clairol makeover. Jesus was unquestionably a hiker who sweated and got dirty. One of the things certainly transmitted on a backpacking trip with youth is that signing on with Jesus means holy alignment with this world, this earth, this piece of *terra firma*; not some ephemeral reunion with Christ in the clouds after we all die. "The whole earth is full of your glory," sing the seraphim during the call of Isaiah (Isa 6:3). It's difficult to compartmentalize faith to a day or certain place in this setting.

"Luke was perhaps a physician," I tell them around the fire. "His Gospel is filled with stories and warnings about wealth and

3. Dean, *Almost Christian*, 24.

poverty. Maybe his church community—filled with all sorts of disciples (poor and rich) through the gift of baptism—struggled with those issues and Luke decided to write it all down as a gospel. If Luke was a doctor, wealthier than most, maybe he struggled with money himself."

We begin this first night with the parable of the Rich Fool in Luke 12; a verse at a time, aloud. I ask the youth how many know the story and invite the group to count how many times the rich farmer uses the pronouns "I" or "my" in these verses. *Seven. No, nine!* "What does this tell you about this man?" Catherine, an eighth-grader, says it best: "He's obsessed with himself." This leads into a conversation about how easy it is to get wrapped up in our stuff. How our possessions can possess us. I spell the word "tithe." No one knows it, but we challenge each other to see if we can live on 90 percent. Everybody talks. There is something about a fire that heightens our ability to listen.

We wake up with sore muscles and, after oatmeal and breakfast bars, reflect upon Jesus's seemingly nutty wisdom in Luke 12:22—"Do not worry about your life, what you will eat, or about your body, what you will wear." Allison, a freshman at Winthrop in the fall, thinks awhile and says, "You know, I constantly worry about what I wear. If I stopped it would free up a lot of my time." I invite the group to think about Allison's comment throughout the day on the trail and ponder an additional thought: *Free up time for what?* "If less time is spent on our personal bodies," Zach mentions at lunch, "maybe that will free up time to care for the Body of Christ, the church."

Water is the topic of conversation as we hike downstream in South Carolina heat and rising humidity, the trail hugging the river, revealing breathtaking cataracts viewed nowhere else but here. We talk about the importance of potable water and community wells and the distance many families walk to get water in developing countries. And we come to Pigpen Falls.

I don't know the story behind the naming of this place, but the image fits as our group sheds packs and throws dirty bodies into cold, bracing water at the base. John, a sixth-grader, finds a pocket of air behind the water flow at the top of the falls and immerses his head for what seems like an inhuman amount of time. One of our adult leaders, Tom, shouts, "Remember your baptism!" Nobody seems worried about their clothing, per Jesus's suggestion. Filling water bottles for the next leg, there is a sudden stillness in the group that suggests we will never again turn on a water faucet at home the way we did three days ago.

Late that afternoon we pile into a shady camp along a winding creek in rhododendron and hemlock, the latter slowly dying in much of eastern North America. After pasta, our text is Luke 14:12–14, Jesus's counsel to invite the poor, crippled, lame, and blind to our meals. We go around the circle and tally pledges for the hike. Almost a thousand dollars has been raised for the hungry. We talk about how this will be used and ponder how we might help in the future. We make the sign of the cross and share bread, wine, and song in waning light, communion made even holier on this trail because of those now joined to us from around the world.

Now I'm standing on the high dive in the middle of the lake at Oconee State Park—end of the trail; pick-up drivers waiting to ferry us back to town. Many of the youth are down below in the water. "Jump, Pastor Frank! You can do it!" Earlier this morning, before hiking the last four miles to the park, we studied a familiar figure from their Bible School days: Zacchaeus, the wee man in Luke 19 who gave half his possessions to the poor after meeting Jesus. He climbed to a wooded vantage point and everything changed.

The high dive affords an incredible view of the lake and mountains we've just hiked through. We too have all been changed during this trip—by Jesus and by his own wooded vantage point, the cross. The sign with which we've been forever marked in baptism. I jump toward the shouts of the family of God waiting below, eager for the water to surround me.

Bibliography

Balmer, Randall. *Growing Pains: Learning to Love My Father's Faith*. Grand Rapids: Brazos, 2001.

Breen, Tom. *The Messiah Formerly Known as Jesus: Dispatches from the Intersection of Christianity and Pop Culture*. Waco, TX: Baylor University Press, 2008.

Dean, Kenda Creasy. *Almost Christian: What the Faith of our Teenagers is Telling the American Church*. New York: Oxford University Press, 2010.

———. "Faith, Nice and Easy: The Almost-Christian Formation of Teens." *Christian Century* (August 10, 2010) 22–27.

Earley, Tony. *Somehow Form a Family: Stories That Are Mostly True*. Chapel Hill: Algonquin, 2001.

Frazier, Ian. "Hungry Minds: Tales from a Chelsea Soup Kitchen." *The New Yorker* (May 26, 2008) 56–65.

Hirsch, Kathleen. "Glimpse of the Holy." *Christian Century* (November 29, 2011) 10–11.

Hoffman, Paul E. *Faith Forming Faith: Bringing New Christians to Baptism and Beyond*. Eugene, OR: Cascade, 2012.

Honeycutt, Frank G. "Eventual Grace: The Long Path to Reconciliation." *Christian Century* (March 7, 2012) 12–13.

———. "Our 50 Father's Days." *The Lutheran* (June 2006) 26–27.

Kellerman, Bill Wylie, ed. *A Keeper of the Word: Selected Writings of William Stringfellow*. Grand Rapids: Eerdmans, 1996.

Kidder, Tracy. *Strength in What Remains*. New York: Random House, 2009.

Lewis, C. S. *The Screwtape Letters*. New York: Bantam, 1982.

Radosh, Daniel. "The Good Book Business: Why Publishers Love the Bible." *The New Yorker* (November 18, 2006) 54–59.

Rudnick, Paul. "Confessions of a Pilgrim Shopaholic." *The New Yorker* (March 16, 2009) 56.

Suttle, Tim. "How to Shrink Your Church." *The Huffington Post* (November 21, 2011). Online: http//www.huffingtonpost.com/tim-suttle/how-to-shrink-your-chur_b_1095841.html.

Udall, Brady. *The Miracle Life of Edgar Mint*. New York: Vintage, 2001.

Wallis, Jim. *The Call to Conversion: Recovering the Gospel for These Times*. San Francisco: Harper Collins, 1992.

www.ingramcontent.com/pod-product-compliance
Lightning Source LLC
LaVergne TN
LVHW051014080826
845145LV00009B/2626